A ROPE OF SAND

A ROPE OF SAND

The AFL-CIO Committee on Political Education, 1955-1967

Alan Draper

PRAEGER

New York
Westport, Connecticut
London

Library of Congress Cataloging-in-Publication Data

Draper, Alan.
   A rope of sand : the AFL-CIO Committee on Political Education,
  1955-1967 / Alan Draper.
     p. cm.
   Bibliography: p.
   Includes index.
   ISBN 0-275-93045-9 (alk. paper)
   1. AFL-CIO. Committee on Political Education—History. 2. AFL-CIO—
Political activity—History. 3. Trade-unions—United States—
Political activity—History—20th century. I. Title.
HD6510.D73 1989
322'.2'0973—dc19   88-11773

Copyright © 1989 by Alan Draper

Library of Congress Catalog Card Number: 88-11773
ISBN: 0-275-93045-9

First published in 1989

Praeger Publishers, One Madison Avenue, New York, NY 10010
A division of Greenwood Press, Inc.

Printed in the United States of America

The paper used in this book complies with the
Permanent Paper Standard issued by the National
Information Standards Organization (Z39.48-1984).

10 9 8 7 6 5 4 3 2 1

Contents

Tables

Acknowledgements

This book examines the history of the Committee on Political Education (COPE), the AFL-CIO's political arm, from its origin in 1955 to the decline of the liberal Democratic coalition in the 1966 midterm elections. In the course of the research and writing of this book, my feelings changed frequently about the material I found. At times, COPE's significance was apparent to me and I saw this book as an attempt to rescue COPE from a lack of appreciation it did not deserve. COPE's work to organize registration-and-vote drives, distribute leaflets, or check voter-registration lists may not be the stuff of great political drama, but it is critical to any electoral campaign. Its work in the trenches of political life on behalf of political and social rights for all Americans deserved to be applauded and recognized. In the same vein I was filled with admiration of COPE for its support of the civil rights movement. COPE has never received the credit it deserved for its contribution to the struggle for black equality though, at the time, it took more than its share of blows for its support.

But there were times when the material left me cynical about labor politics. At such moments, COPE appeared as an underachiever to me; hollow and pitiable when measured against the potential of trade union political mobilization, or its success elsewhere. I then came to believe that the purpose of this book was to convince readers that there was *less* to COPE than met the eye. Needless to say, I did not find such a task exhilarating. Fortunately, there was enough evidence of the former sort to convince me that this view was not completely true. Readers, however, must decide for themselves which perspective holds the greater truth.

While my feelings about the material fluctuated, what remained steady and kept me on course was the help I received along the way. Professor Mark Kesselman of Columbia University provided both guidance and friendship. If this book is clear and informative it is only because the qualities of his work have rubbed off on my own. While I am no longer Mark's student, I will always consider him my mentor.

I owe a debt also to Professors Richard Guarasci, Fred Exoo, and Ansil Ramsay of the Department of Government at St. Lawrence University. In different ways, each has challenged me, and I am grateful that they have chosen to share their good sense with me. Professor Robert Schwartz of the Department of History at St. Lawrence University and my racetrack buddy read the complete manuscript. His tips on ways to improve the book's argument, and on American labor history in general, were much better than the tips he offered on horses. There were times though, when I must confess, I wished it was the other way around. Another colleague from the Department of History, Professor Lawrence Baron, also read the complete manuscript. He offered cogent criticism and welcome encouragement in just the right proportions. Errors of judgement that appear in the text are my responsibility and are likely the result of failing to take my colleagues' good advice.

I would also like to thank Gail Colvin and Laurie Olmstead who patiently and expertly prepared the manuscript. I appreciate the yeoman work Sheila Murphy has done for me as departmental secretary. Robert Dinwiddie was an indispensable guide to the fine collection at the Southern Labor Archives, Georgia State University, Atlanta, Georgia. I would also like to thank archivists at the following collections that I made use of in my research: the Southern History Collection at the Library of the University of North Carolina, Chapel Hill, North Carolina; the George Meany Memorial Archives in Silver Springs, Maryland; the Robert F. Wagner Labor Archives at the Tamiment Institute in New York City; and the Southern Regional Council Collection at Atlanta University Library Center, Atlanta, Georgia. While on the topic of archives, let me say a word about the endnotes. In the course of my initial research for this book I had access to the private papers of Dan Powell and Philip Weightman while these were still in their possession. They have since been placed in archives and inventoried. I went back to the material when it was placed in archives to locate the appropriate box and folder numbers of the material I used. In a few cases I was unable to locate this material in the archival collection. Thus, in a rare instance or two, some citations in the endnotes are incomplete.

For the last 15 years I have benefitted from the friendship of a group of very special people. Just as Mark Twain or Bruce Springsteen would have predicted, I learned more from my friends than I did from any school. Some of us met as undergraduates at the University of Wisconsin, and we all shared a passion for basketball and socialism. Debates on the relative merits of shooters *vs* scorers rivaled those of the most abstruse Marxology. I have always considered myself lucky to share their company and friendship. I owe an enormous debt to Jeffrey Burstein, Gary Borenstein, Edward Edelman, Larry Engelstein, Lester Lannon, Walter Malakoff, Joshua Tankel, and Bryan Winston. A special thanks, though, to Don Palmer, another member of the Wisconsin crowd. He has been a special friend to me and I respect him tremendously. It pains me though to reveal this publicly to him because this will ruin the image of a tough guy that I have cultivated over the years. It makes no difference that I know he saw through this thin disguise years ago.

I have especially benefitted from the love, humor, and encouragement of my wife, Jacqueline. She is truly my better half. If Sisyphus had had such a mate he wouldn't have seen his task as such a burden. My son, Sam, also deserves mention for arriving late enough to let me complete this book.

My greatest debt, however, is to my family. My parents, Robert and Clarice, and my brother, Douglas, have had to suffer me the longest. Marx spoke of unequal exchange between workers and employers, but he failed to mention that the greatest unequal exchange occurs within families. This book is dedicated to my family in the hope that it will begin to correct the balance sheet between us.

"The Federation had to win men by the authority of sound logic and results. It had less authority than national trade unions, for it was the voluntary banding together of those autonomous unions. Its continuous existence depended upon mutual service and welfare. It was at once a rope of sand and yet the strongest human force—a voluntary association united by common need and held together by mutual self-interest."

Samuel Gompers,
Seventy Years of Life and Labor: An Autobiography

A ROPE OF SAND

Introduction

Trade unions in Western Europe have either created or identified themselves with left-wing parties while American unions have not. Social scientists have offered a variety of reasons to explain the failure of American trade unions to follow the example of their European counterparts.[1] It has been argued that affluence and opportunities for social mobility prevented strong feelings of class identification from emerging among American workers. American trade unions faithfully reflected the entrepreneurial spirit of their members and were thus never inclined toward socialism.[2] Another argument has been that ethnic loyalties divided the working class. Workplace conflicts between employers and employees were not reflected in the community at large where ethnic loyalties remained the basis of identification and organization. As a result, workplace conflicts did not overlap or coincide with conflicts that existed outside of work. Trade unionism was thus confined to narrow issues of wages and working conditions. Ethnic politics and pure and simple trade unionism emerged together.[3] Finally, Louis Hartz suggests that socialism failed to take root in the American working class and their unions because the U.S. lacked a feudal past. Feudalism provided European workers with a corporate image of society which made them more amenable to socialist ideas. American workers, on the other hand, born capitalist, rejected socialist collectivism in favor of Lockean individualism.[4]

Taken collectively or individually these arguments are compelling reasons for the failure of American workers and the unions they formed to support and identify themselves with socialist political parties. But these arguments also have an abstract, ahistorical quality to them because they assume that the failure of American unions to identify themselves with socialist political parties needs to be explained. The very question "Why No Socialism in the U.S.?" presumes an historical outcome and treats the politics of American trade unions as deviations from that point. Worse, so much effort is spent trying to explain why American trade unions did not behave politically as they should have, that what American trade unions have done politically has received little attention at all. In 1963 Harry Scoble lamented that when "one searches the literature of social science for a full description of what it is in fact that labor unions do in elections and for systematic analysis of such activity, one finds pronouncements and sentiments instead of facts and science."[5]

Curiously, when social scientists did turn their attention to American trade union political behavior they discovered that American trade unions did not act altogether differently from their West European counterparts. The argument that the American labor movement is different or exceptional may have been taken too far. Katznelson writes:

> The term "American exceptionalism" is often used as if it provided a self-evident explanation. But its meaning is hardly obvious because the American experience is not as exceptional as conventionally thought. If the issue is Sombart's, there was a significant socialist movement in America, especially in the period in which he wrote....And if the issue of American exceptionalism hinges on Lenin's distinction between revolutionary and trade union consciousness, then the United States is quite typical. Nowhere in the West has the proletariat lived up to Lenin's revolutionary standard....Nor is the issue of American exceptionalism one of the absence of class related conflict....Labor organizing disputes, violent strikes...community based land use and school conflicts...have been characteristic features of the pattern of class conflict and disequilibrium in American capitalism. In all of these ways, the United States does not seem qualitatively different from other Western capitalist societies.[6]

Differences between West European and American labor movements may be more a matter of degree than of kind. This view has been articulated by analysts Michael Harrington and J. David Greenstone, who argue that the American labor movement resembles West European social democratic movements in the legislative goals it pursues and in its efforts to achieve them. Greenstone writes "In the policy process, the American labor movement supports the continuous expansion of welfare state measures. In national electoral politics, the unions have assumed many of the functions of the political campaign apparatus for the Democrats, the dominant party in the United States since 1930."[7]

First, Greenstone argues that the programmatic objectives of the AFL-CIO are typical social democratic policy concerns. The AFL-CIO pursues what Greenstone calls consumer-class demands: legislation to protect consumers and the environment as well as social welfare legislation for the economically and socially disadvantaged. Support for such policies is evidence of the AFL-CIO's social democratic character because these policies confer benefits on groups beyond the union membership: clean air and Medicare are for all workers regardless of whether they are union members or not. By defining the interests of its members so broadly, the AFL-CIO includes nonunion workers and minorities, groups that also have an interest in consumer-class demands, within its political constituency. By pursuing these consumer-class demands the AFL-CIO defines the interests of its members in class terms, beyond the common organizational affiliation that all trade union members share. The AFL-CIO represents the interests of its members as citizens, not simply as workers.

The second way in which the political activity of the AFL-CIO is said to be typically social democratic is in its relationship to political parties. The AFL-CIO acts as a campaign arm of the Democratic party, supplying it with money and using its organizational resources on behalf of Democratic party candidates. The AFL-CIO not only defines its political constituency in class as opposed to interest group terms, but it seeks to mobilize this broad class into the Democratic party. In functional terms, the AFL-CIO-Democratic party linkage resembles union-party linkages found in social democratic movements throughout Western Europe. Greenstone writes:

> In the early and mid-1960s, the American labor movement's role in the national Democratic party represented a partial equivalence to the Social Democratic (formerly Socialist) party-trade union alliance in much of Western Europe. This equivalence obtained with respect to its activities as a party campaign (and lobbying) organization, its influence as a party faction, and its welfare state objectives.[8]

The purpose of this book is to investigate the degree to which the AFL-CIO has forged a constituency with an interest in social democratic objectives and has mobilized this constituency to pursue these objectives through the Democratic party. That is, to what extent has the AFL-CIO forged a social democratic constituency within the Democratic party?

The organization that operates as the political arm of the AFL-CIO is the Committee on Political Education (COPE). This book will examine the work of COPE from its inception in 1955 to the devastating defeat of COPE-endorsed candidates in the 1966 congressional elections to see whether the AFL-CIO's political activity conforms to the social democratic model. As the title of COPE suggests, this organization is concerned with the political education of AFL-CIO members. COPE is also supposed to organize registration and get-out-the-vote drives, contribute money and other forms of assistance to labor-endorsed candidates, and coordinate political activity among AFL-CIO affiliated unions and their locals. In addition, although the affiliated unions are free to endorse candidates, COPE's endorsements at the national, state and local levels represent organized labor. COPE does not lobby for legislation favorable to trade unions, nor does it determine AFL-CIO policy positions. Rather, its task can be described best as "contact work" with the rank and file: political education and voter assistance to ensure that organized labor has allies in political office.

An examination of COPE will help us assess the social democratic character of organized labor more than the study of any single union's political activity. Unlike the affiliated unions that reflect the political interests of workers in a particular trade or industry, COPE must condense the political interests of union members across the various trades and industries. As the political arm of the AFL-CIO—labor's peak organization—COPE is in an organizational position to take a more generalized view of the interests of union members than any affiliated union. If COPE does not broadly define the political interests of union members in class terms, then one is unlikely to find such evidence among the affiliated unions.

Other parts of the AFL-CIO organization, such as the legislative department that lobbies on behalf of policies supported by the AFL-CIO, may also express a social democratic perspective through their activity. But their ability to lobby for social democratic demands will be ineffective if COPE has not already fashioned a constituency to support these objectives through the Democratic party. Success in the legislature is dependent on success in the hustings. COPE's contribution is thus critical.

The degree to which trade unions pursue social democratic demands through a political party depends upon the conflict strategy a labor movement adopts. The term 'conflict strategy' refers to the actions labor movements take to press their distributive claims upon society. Labor movements pursue the redistribution of social wealth through either collective bargaining at the level of the economy or through legislation at the level of the state. That is, they pursue the redistribution of the national income by pursuing their claims either in the economic arena through a display of market power or in the political arena by attempting to gain state power. These alternatives are referred to as the market and political strategy, respectively. Of course, every labor movement pursues both market and political strategies simultaneously, but the particular mix of strategies within each labor movement is distinctive. Whether labor movements adopt a market or political strategy—each with their appropriate trade union structures—will determine the degree to which trade unions behave in a social democratic manner: define the political interests of their members in class terms and forge extensive links with political parties.

Labor movements that adopt a political strategy are more likely to have centralized trade union structures that permit them to act in a social democratic manner than labor movements that follow a market strategy. As Lenin well knew, organizational forms are not innocent in their political consequences.[9] Centralized federations have the resources and authority to pursue issues beyond the narrow market concerns of the affiliated unions. They tend to define the political interests of their members in class terms in order to create as wide a base of support as possible for the party to which they are allied. Trade unions realize that the electoral success of these parties is essential if the labor movement's political strategy is to succeed in extracting social benefits from the state. Moreover, Stephens found that the more decision making and resources were concentrated at the top, the greater "the opinion making and political capabilities" of the trade union movement.[10] Centralized federations are able to accumulate resources for political activity that are beyond the bounds of any single affiliate or decentralized federation to supply, and have the authority to coordinate and direct political programs that weak federations lack.

Market-oriented labor movements, on the other hand, tend toward administratively decentralized trade union structures. They lack the authority to intervene in the internal affairs of their affiliates and the resources to pursue objectives independent of them. This decentralization of authority and resources limits the degree to which the national federation can pursue demands that are not related directly to the collective bargaining interests of the affiliated unions. Indeed, this is the case with COPE. Due to the decentralization of authority and resources within the AFL-CIO, COPE is organizationally dependent on the affiliated and local union leadership to carry out its various programs. COPE cannot compel their participation in its register-and-vote drives, its voter education programs, or its efforts to raise money on behalf of endorsed candidates. If COPE is to elicit the cooperation and support from them that it requires to be successful, COPE must satisfy the self-interest of the affiliated and local union leadership. The self-interest of this group lies in its demands which pertain to the institutional security and autonomy of trade unions, and not in social democratic demands. While Greenstone is correct when he argues that the secondary leadership has an interest in social democratic demands because they confer benefits on all union members regardless of which union they belong to, he fails to appreciate that the secondary leadership has no incentive to pursue such issues. Following a market strategy, union contracts already provide benefits, such as health care and pensions, that the rank and file would receive from welfare state legislation. With regard to issues of institutional security and autonomy, however, the secondary leadership has both an interest and incentive to pursue such demands. These issues affect the performance of their unions in collective bargaining. Inasmuch as the job tenure and career goals of the secondary leadership depend upon their performance in collective bargaining they would be responsive to these types of issues.

Faced with these organizational constraints—COPE's dependence on the affiliated and local union leadership for cooperation and support—COPE did little to educate the membership to the social democratic agenda that the AFL-CIO was pursuing in Congress during the 1960s. COPE was organizationally dependent on the international and local union leadership who had little incentive to educate their members to social democratic demands or to support endorsed candidates on this basis. As Selznick found with the TVA, COPE's need to satisfy other institutions that it depended upon for success altered and constrained its activity.[11] Ultimately, it was the labor movement's market strategy which dictated its decentralized structure that was so constraining.

Ideological support for the Democratic party's program of expanding the welfare state and providing consumer protection was only one of the ways that COPE's activity allegedly resembled social democratic behavior. According to Greenstone and Harrington, COPE not only provided ideological support for the broad, consumer-class goals of the Democratic party, but rendered organizational support to it as well. Here, both analysts are on firmer ground. COPE financially supported Democratic party candidates. More important, it sought to increase the voting participation of traditional Democratic supporters. For example, COPE conducted register-and-vote drives among groups outside the AFL-CIO membership, such as minorities, in order to increase the total Democratic party vote. This evidence supports the social democratic surrogate thesis.

Greenstone claims that COPE's partisan identification with the Democrats began in the 1930s when the unions redefined their members' interests to include social democratic demands. "Given this new broader definition of union interests, support for the Democrats and the welfare state followed rather automatically."[12] But Greenstone misidentifies that aspect of the New Deal that drove the unions into alliance with the Democrats. More important than the breakthrough in social legislation that the New Deal introduced was the politicization of labor relations that it promoted. It was the latter, more than the former, which led American unions to ally with the Democratic party.

Prior to the New Deal, the American Federation of Labor (AFL) adhered to the philosophy of voluntarism. Voluntarism held that state interference or regulation of labor relations was unjustified and counterproductive. But with a sympathetic administration in Washington, D.C. and the organization of the Congress of Industrial Organizations (CIO) in the 1930s, organized labor adopted a new attitude towards the regulation of labor relations. It would now try to secure bargaining rights through politics rather than against it. It would now try to direct and control legislation concerning the collective bargaining rights of trade unions rather than simply condemn political regulation as unwarranted political interference.

The new strategy of securing bargaining rights through politics would pay dividends only if labor was politically powerful. But following World War II the political fortunes of organized labor were to decline not improve. As the unions discovered with the passage of the Taft-Hartley

Act in 1947 and President Dwight D. Eisenhower's appointment of an unsympathetic National Labor Relations Board (NLRB), the politicization of labor relations—which the unions had viewed so favorably during the New Deal—could be used to restrict the bargaining rights of trade unions as well as advance them. Ironically, the politicization of labor relations introduced by the New Deal had become an opening through which antilabor legislators could now threaten union security. In order to secure their organizational rights from legislative attack, the unions sought closer relations with the Democratic party. They identified the security of their collective bargaining rights with the political success of the Democratic party. With their institutional security at stake, organized labor aggregated voters into the Party and gave it financial support to help the Party succeed politically.

The AFL-CIO did not identify themselves with the Democratic party to pursue consumer-class demands as Greenstone suggests. Rather, its linkages were motivated by more defensive concerns: to protect the market strategy of the affiliated unions in a period when the legal and economic conditions surrounding collective bargaining had been politicized.

This book will be structured in the following manner. Chapter 1 will present a short history of unions in American politics from 1906 to 1940. At the beginning of the century, the political behavior of the AFL was guided by the philosophy of voluntarism. The AFL opposed social legislation as well as government interference in labor relations. Organized labor was sympathetic to the Democratic party but offered the Party only token amounts of assistance. The politicization of labor relations introduced by the New Deal, however, brought changes in organized labor's relationship to political parties.

Chapter 2 discusses the postwar strategy and political activity of the AFL and CIO up until their merger in 1955. Between 1945 and 1955, unions found the political influence upon which they had staked their abandonment of voluntarism eluding them. The passage of antilabor legislation that restricted the market power of unions drove both the CIO and AFL to seek closer relations with the Democratic party. Finally the threat to union security loomed so large that the AFL and CIO agreed to merge even though important issues that had hamstrung previous negotiations had not been resolved. As a result of merger, the AFL and CIO combined their separate political organizations to form COPE. By merging their separate political organizations in COPE, the AFL and CIO hoped to protect the affiliated unions from new restrictive labor legislation and the unsympathetic administration of existing labor laws.

Chapter 3 reviews the organization of COPE. This chapter will demonstrate that COPE is not a "well oiled political machine,"[13] but is in organizational disarray. COPE committees at the state and local levels are understaffed, underfunded, and powerless to coordinate and provide political direction to the affiliated locals. At the local union level, COPE committees are not enthusiastically supported by the local union leadership, and when they do exist fail to function year-round. Responsibility for this disorganization rests, ultimately, with the decentralized structure that the AFL-CIO's market strategy requires. The decentralization of resources and authority within the AFL-CIO ensures the affiliated unions that COPE will service their collective bargaining needs as opposed to broader, ideological class concerns.

Chapters 4 and 5 will present our case study of COPE from 1955 to 1967. Material for these chapters is drawn from COPE's records, interviews with and access to the private papers of former COPE staff people, AFL-CIO and COPE publications, AFL-CIO and state AFL-CIO convention proceedings, and published reports of COPE activities in the press. This material provides a "best case" test of COPE's social democratic activities. The communications the COPE national office received from the field describe the work of the most politically active sections of the AFL-CIO. Thus, our sources provide a description of COPE activities at their best to educate and mobilize not only AFL-CIO members but the broader constituency of the Democratic party, and the problems COPE encountered in this regard.

Chapter 4 describes how threats to union security sparked voter aggregation activity on behalf of the Democratic party. COPE first began a national drive to organize voters beyond the AFL-CIO membership into the Democratic party in the 1960 election. This followed the passage of the Landrum-Griffin Act in 1959 which the AFL-CIO opposed vehemently. The further politicization of labor relations introduced by the Landrum-Griffin Act not only compelled COPE to organize voters on behalf of the Democratic party, but it also increased the commitment of the affiliated unions to COPE as well. For the first time, the building trades unions contributed more than token amounts to COPE and participated in COPE register-and-vote drives.

Chapter 5 argues that COPE did little to educate its membership—or anyone else—to the social democratic demands the Democratic party and AFL-CIO leadership advocated in Congress. But COPE did follow a partisan strategy that drew it closer to the Democratic party. COPE assisted the Party through the register-and-vote drives it conducted among minority groups. COPE's efforts to bring these voters to the polls expanded the Democratic party constituency and the turnout for Democratic party candidates. But the secondary labor leadership, especially local union leaders, were reluctant to participate in such activity. COPE was forced to become a silent partner to groups it wanted to bring into the Democratic party because of the skepticism its strategy encountered from lower levels of the labor bureaucracy. In 1966 COPE paid the price for its silence. Because COPE did little to involve the secondary leadership in the coalition it was forging at the national level or to educate them to the social democratic goals it was pursuing, the membership fell victim to a backlash against Great Society programs in the 1966 congressional elections.

In conclusion, the social democracy of the AFL-CIO was not

transmitted ideologically to the membership by educating them to the consumer-class goals the Democratic party and AFL-CIO leadership advocated in Congress. Organizationally, however, COPE did act in a partisan manner when it organized groups outside the AFL-CIO membership into the Democratic party. But it had to bypass the secondary labor leadership who showed little interest in such activity to do so. No wonder Harrington describes the political activity of the AFL-CIO as "an invisible mass movement" for social democracy.[14] It all occurred without the participation and involvement of the membership; it literally occurred above their heads.

Will the American labor movement continue to adhere to a market strategy which has shaped COPE's approach and effectiveness? Labor leaders do not adopt strategies arbitrarily, but "choose" strategies that are appropriate given the conditions they encounter. The conditions that made a market strategy appropriate for the American labor movement are eroding. Whether the American labor movement will adopt a new strategy more congruent with the challenges and circumstances it faces today remains, however, an open question.

NOTES

1. The literature on American exceptionalism is voluminous. For a selection of relevant material on this issue see the essays by Eric Foner, "Why is There No Socialism in the United States?" *History Workshop Journal* 17: 57-80; Sean Wilentz, "Against Exceptionalism: Class Consciousness and the American Labor Movement, 1790-1920," *International Labor and Working Class History* No. 26, (Fall 1984): 1-24; and Seymour Martin Lipset, "Why No Socialism in the U.S.?" in S. Bialer and S. Sluzar, eds. *Sources of Contemporary Radicalism* (Boulder, Colorado: Westview Press, 1977), 31-151.

2. Werner Sombart, *Why is There No Socialism in the United States?* (White Plains, NY: Sharpe Publishers, 1976).

3. Susan Hirsh, *Roots of the American Working Class: The Industrialization of Crafts in Newark, 1800-1860* (Philadelphia: University of Pennsylvania Press, 1978).

4. Louis Hartz, *The Liberal Tradition in America* (New York: Harcourt, Brace & World, 1955).

5. Harry M. Scoble, "Organized Labor in Electoral Politics: The State of the Discipline," *Western Political Quarterly* Vol. 14, (September 1963): 666.

6. Ira Katznelson, "Considerations on Social Democracy in the United States," *Comparative Politics* Vol. 11, (October 1978): 95.

7. J. David Greenstone, *Labor in American Politics*, 2nd ed. (Chicago: University of Chicago Press, 1977), 4.

8. Ibid., 361-62.

9. Vladimir Lenin, *What Is To Be Done?* (New York: International Publishers, 1973).

10. John D. Stephens, "Class Formation and Class Consciousness: A Theoretical and Empirical Analysis with Reference to Britain and Sweden," *British Journal of Sociology* Vol. 30, (December 1979): 399.

11. Philip Selznick, *T.V.A. and the Grass Roots* (Berkeley: University of California Press, 1949).

12. Greenstone, xxiv.

13. Harry Holloway, "Interest Groups in the Post-Partisan Era: The Political Machine of the AFL-CIO," *Political Science Quarterly* Vol. 94, (Spring 1979): 133.

14. Michael Harrington, *Socialism* (New York: Saturday Review Press, 1973), 305-31.

1. Labor Politics in Historical Perspective

All labor movements follow both economic and political strategies simultaneously. They pursue their goal of redistribution through the exercise of market and political power. What is distinctive about the American labor movement, however, is the degree to which it has organized and mobilized itself for conflict in the economic as opposed to political arena. Its particular mix of strategies is skewed toward the economic struggle. This market commitment is expressed by Mitchell Sviridorf, former president of the Connecticut state AFL-CIO. "Better than Gompers's 'reward your friends and punish your enemies' is another quotation that more accurately reflects the mood of the American labor movement. 'Economic organization and control of economic power are the fulcrums that make possible influence and power in every relationship.'"[1]

Factors such as the lack of a revolutionary tradition, the opportunities available for social mobility, the presence of ethnic cleavages within the working class, and institutional obstacles to political reform may have led labor leaders to adopt a market strategy but they did not settle the issue. Rather, American labor leaders vacillated constantly between market and political approaches. Rehmus writes, "In one sense, the history of the American labor movement can be viewed as a record of conflict between leaders who stressed the importance of political activity versus those who argued the primacy of obtaining economic gains for wage earners."[2] The market strategy that the labor movement finally adopted was a source of intense conflict and debate within it. Norman Ware observed, "While it is assumed today that collective bargaining is the major function of a labor union, it took nearly a century of agitation and experiment to reach this conclusion."[3] Options were open and choices had to be made. Even during the 1920s when the unions seemed most in thrall to a market strategy, this strategy was not completely successful in winning over the membership or in determining the pattern of trade union behavior. It appealed to only a limited constituency within the working class. But this constituency was able to develop traditions and precedents that sanctified the market strategy, organize unions in accord with its administrative requirements, and successfully defend it.

VOLUNTARISM

The market strategy was codified in the philosophy of voluntarism to which the unions adhered. Voluntarism did not develop from deep sociological reflection but from more mundane and practical considerations. Perlman and Taft write, "The voluntarism or anti-governmentalism of the Gompers group was not the result of an assiduous study of Herbert Spencer, but of Attorney General Olney's invoking the Sherman Anti-trust law and Interstate Commerce law against striking railway men."[4] It was the philosophy of an organization that denied it was motivated by philosophical principles. In his book *The Labor Philosophy of Samuel Gompers*, Louis Reed describes voluntarism thusly:

> Society is made up of contending groups, each of which has an eye single to its own interests. Labor is one of these groups. It alone understands its interests and ought to be left free to advance them. Hence, what the workers chiefly demand of society is recognition of their rights to form unions, to strike, to boycott, etc. As with labor so with the rest—progress will be made if each group follows its own self-interest without regard to the others. For the government to interfere in this struggle is wrong and harmful; wrong because such interference is destructive of personal (and inalienable) rights, harmful because it destroys initiative and self-reliance.[5]

Voluntarism expresses a profound distrust of the state. Legislative remedies are inferior to the benefits individuals can achieve through their own collective action because such legislation presumably robs people of initiative and responsibility, government is not as knowledgeable about the needs of individuals as their voluntary organizations and, finally, legislation promotes "big government" under which people lose their independence and freedom. Thus, according to voluntarist ideas, the state should not interfere with the exclusive right of unions to represent workers in areas covered by collective bargaining agreements. Neither should the state provide welfare state benefits or workplace protection to the working class. This type of legislation competes with the efforts of unions that could better provide similar benefits to their members through collective bargaining.

While skeptical of the value of political activity in general, voluntarism does approve of political action that removes legislative restrictions which inhibit the ability of organizations to pursue their member's interests. With regard to unions, such legislation might include restrictions on "the freedom of men to form unions and to pursue such tactics as the strike, boycott, and picketing...."[6] Karson found that during the early years of the AFL, "The main legislation which the Federation desired was of a kind restraining the state from limiting the economic power inherent in trade unionism."[7] A union inhibited by legislation that restricts organizing or strikes or boycotts cannot adequately represent the interests of its members. For this reason voluntarism approves of political activity to remove these constraints.

Distrustful of benefits derived from legislation and finding virtue in the benefits members win through collective effort, voluntarism was a philosophical justification of the market strategy. Selig Perlman argues that the American labor movement was attracted to this philosophy because voluntarism was in harmony with American conditions. According to Perlman, "the AFL grasped the idea, supremely correct for American conditions, that the economic front was the only front in which the labor army could stay united."[8] Perlman claims voluntarism was appropriate for the American labor movement because it took into account the degree to which the institution of private property was entrenched within American society. This limited the degree of radicalism the community would tolerate from trade unions. Second, Perlman cites the lack of class consciousness among American workers. Lastly, Perlman argues voluntarism was appropriate because the structure of government, with its innumerable points of access through which obdurate minorities could block reform, made it difficult for workers to win benefits from the state.

Reed supports Perlman fully. He claims that voluntarism would have become the dominant philosophy within the AFL independent of Gompers's articulate and vigorous defense of it. He writes, "For looking back, it seems positive that it was only upon these principles: action upon the economic field, no independent activity, no alternatives, in fact, no 'ideas' whatever beyond wages and hours that unionism could have developed in this country at this period."[9]

Both Perlman and Reed are undoubtedly correct that political and ideological factors militated against a more political strategy being pursued by American trade unions. But this explanation is too sweeping. In this guise, voluntarism appears as the inevitable verdict of history when, in fact, its advocates were hard pressed to defend it. Socialist trade unionists within the AFL opposed voluntarism vigorously and their viewpoint was only narrowly defeated at AFL conventions.[10] Moreover, Fink found that at state and local levels "labor leaders advocated a program of legislated social reform approximating the welfare state or guarantor state" which was anathema to voluntarism.[11]

Programs villified by the national leadership, such as unemployment compensation or minimum wage laws, were advocated at state and local levels. It would seem that voluntarism had a narrower constituency than Perlman or Reed would lead us to believe.

One reason why voluntarism was so dominant within the AFL was its function as an "organizational ideology protecting the craft union officials of the AFL."[12] The much vaunted practicality and appropriateness of voluntarism lay not in its "fit" with American conditions, but in the instrumental purposes it served a trade union leadership interested in organizational maintenance.

Voluntarism legitimated "the power of the craft union internationals and...the power of the leadership both within the Federation and within the internationals themselves."[13] The limited role voluntarism accorded the state in labor relations preserved the domain and autonomy of affiliated union leaders. Their activity would not be constrained by state regulation. Moreover, according to the tenets of voluntarism, compulsion by the central labor federation was construed to be as harmful as compulsion by the state. Neither was an expression of group interest, like the affiliated unions, that arose spontaneously from society. The central federation was therefore to be kept weak, without authority to coerce the affiliated unions. Affiliated union leaders supported voluntarism because it precluded interference from the state or the central labor federation and left them free to manage their affairs as they saw fit.

Organizational reasons motivated affiliated union leaders to oppose social legislation as vehemently as they did state regulation of labor-management relations. Trade union leaders feared that social legislation would weaken the ties of loyalty between workers and their unions. Another fear of social legislation that union leaders had was that it would minimize their function within the union. Their collective bargaining expertise would not be as indispensable to their members if social benefits were also available through the state. Social legislation was thought to not only pose a threat to the loyalty members had to their unions, but to the career requirements of trade union officials as well.[14]

But the success of voluntarism cannot be attributed solely to the degree it served the organizational interests of the affiliated union leadership. For voluntarism to be as dominant as it was, the membership would have had to subscribe to it too. Union membership at the turn of the century consisted almost exclusively of skilled workers. This group was especially attracted to voluntarism because they still had market power they could employ in group conflict with employers. Technological innovation had not yet affected the position of the skilled trades collectively, nor had the principles of scientific management been diffused widely among industrial managers. The knowledge of production processes that skilled workers possessed made them indispensable and gave them leverage in collective bargaining with employers. As Dawson shows, skilled workers were able to exploit their market power successfully and establish working conditions and a standard of living visibly distinguished from the unskilled.[15]

In addition, skilled workers were attracted to voluntarism because increasingly they found alternatives to it beyond their grasp. The concentration and centralization of production, and the growth of national markets at the turn of the century, rendered a worker's hope of becoming an entrepreneur obsolete.   With the growth of trusts, no alternative for skilled workers was viable other than to ruthlessly exploit whatever leverage in the market they had.   Skilled workers turned to voluntarism and its idea of group conflict at the level of the economy once they accepted the permanency of their status as wage labor.

As growing concentration and centralization of production narrowed the options of skilled workers, so did the unremitting hostility of the state. The lesson of McKees Rock, Homestead, the Pullman strike, and Coeur d'Alene was that the state was hostile to the interests of workers.   These encounters with the government did not instill confidence in workers that politics was a fruitful arena from which benefits could be derived.   Moreover, the nativist racism of skilled workers precluded an alliance with unskilled immigrant workers that a political strategy would have required.[16]   Finally, in a still predominantly agricultural society, skilled workers composed only a small proportion of the total population.   The contrast between the shopfloor power skilled workers possessed and the lack of political resources such workers could command focused their hopes and ambitions on the workplace rather than the state.

FROM THE AFL TO THE CIO

Between 1900 and 1936 organized labor acted according to its voluntarist principles in the political field. With few exceptions, the AFL abjured social legislation and repeatedly tried to deny the state any role in labor relations.   Its level of political activity rose and fell in conjunction with threats to the collective bargaining interests of unions. The AFL's political activity was limited to defending narrow organizational interests and restricted to activating only its immediate membership. Marc Karson describes the AFL's participation in politics during this period thusly, "If the state power left the AFL alone, the organization was content to pay little attention to politics and rely instead on the potentialities of economic power.   When government behavior was such, however, as to seriously threaten trade union security, the Federation resorted to pressure politics on the two major parties."[17]

In 1906 the AFL took an unprecedented step. It submitted to Congress and the executive a "Bill of Grievances" that detailed the legislative proposals it wished to see enacted but had been disregarded by both branches. High on the AFL's list of demands was relief from court injunctions that prohibited unions from engaging in boycotts and restricted picketing. This was not a new demand. The AFL had lobbied Congress for an anti-injunction bill for more than a decade prior to 1906 but to no avail. The attention of union leaders was concentrated on the need for injunction relief by the Danbury Hatters case in 1902. In this case, the courts upheld a company's suit for damages that stemmed from a union boycott of the company's goods. In 1906 another injunction issued by the courts, this time against an ITU local, raised the ire of union leaders. A strike by the ITU was conducted in an orderly fashion, yet the courts still enjoined the union's activity. Until legislation could rewrite the law and put an end to court injunctions, union security was imperiled.

Rather than alter its balance between economic and political strategies, the AFL decided to try new tactics as a way to meet these challenges. Previously the AFL had only lobbied to advance its legislative program. Now the AFL would, in Gompers's phrase, "stand by our friends and administer a stinging rebuke to men or parties...who are hostile." The first target of the AFL's electoral involvement was Republican Robert Littlefield of Maine. Littlefield sat on the House Judiciary Committee and was a well known opponent of injunction relief bills. AFL officials went to Littlefield's district and tried to mobilize union members against his candidacy. Despite this effort and similar ones in other districts, the Congress that took office in 1906 was no more favorable to AFL demands than previous legislatures had been.

Only when one compares the actions of the AFL to those of British trade unions during this period can one appreciate how moderate and tentative these responses were to the legal challenges that confronted American trade unions. Taff-Vale and related court decisions in Britain posed a threat to the market power of British trade unions in much the same way that American trade unions were challenged. In response to these threats British trade unions threw their support to the nascent Labor party.[18] The response of the AFL, however, was thoroughly pluralistic. The AFL continued to define the interests of its members in terms of the organizational security of the affiliated unions and to confine its political activity to mobilizing its own membership. Although Gompers leaned personally toward the Democratic party, the AFL did not lend the Party sustained campaign support.

World War I forced the AFL to depart temporarily from the *laissez faire* principles of voluntarism. Gompers thought it wiser for labor to claim its share of representation on government boards rather than face the unpleasant alternative of finding those boards staffed by people hostile to labor's interests. But this departure from voluntarism was short-lived. The 1920s saw the unions return to voluntarism in order to again face the challenge of court injunctions. Although the fortunes of the AFL fell to a new low in the 1920s, Gompers reaffirmed the value of voluntarism in his last speech before an AFL convention in 1924. He told the assembled delegates, "I want to say to you men and women of the American labor movement, do not reject the cornerstone upon which labor's structure has been builded [sic]—but base your all upon voluntarist principles....We have tried and proved these principles in economic, social and international relations. They have been tried and not found wanting. Where we have tried other ways we have failed."[19] This advice, however, was unable to stem the decline in union membership and power. In 1924 the AFL had its policy proposals rejected by the platforms of both major parties. As a result, the AFL took the novel step of formally endorsing the third party candidacy of Robert LaFollette who ran on the Progressive party ticket. This was the first official endorsement by the AFL in a presidential campaign. It was forced to take such an unprecedented action more out of despair and disappointment with the indifference and hostility shown to it by Congress and the two major parties than by support for the social reform program of the Progressives.

Earlier in his career, Gompers had argued that one of the virtues of voluntarism was that it permitted labor unions to weather unfavorable economic and political circumstances. Rather than dissipate their energy trying to reverse these conditions, voluntarism counseled a strategy of retreat to the economic power inherent within trade unionism. The organization would be weakened but it would still exist to recover lost ground once prosperity returned. Voluntarism, however, faced its greatest test in the 1930s when the Great Depression caused many to doubt that prosperity would return.

The 1930s were a watershed for American labor. This decade saw the number of unionized workers increase fourfold; unskilled workers were organized into the CIO; and the political activity of American trade unions increased substantially. Greenstone claims that the basic political issue that had aroused union political activity in the past was finally resolved during this decade. "The Wagner Act...represented...the culmination of the long and often frustrating search for organizational security that Gompers had begun in the 1880s."[20] Once assured that their basic organizational rights were legally protected and now representing a broader constituency than simply skilled workers, Greenstone argues that the political objectives of the labor movement expanded to include welfare state measures. Pursuit of these broader class—as opposed to interest group—goals led the unions into alliance with the Democratic party which proceeded to lay the foundation of the American welfare state.[21]

But, "the Lewis-Democratic party coalition was from the first, based on common necessity, not shared values."[22] While it is certainly true that the CIO supported New Deal social legislation, the same objectives that stimulated union political activity in previous decades motivated them in the 1930s: to safeguard the market strategies of the affiliated unions. But changing circumstances now redefined the lengths that unions would have to go to achieve this goal. Far from guaranteeing basic legal rights for trade unions, the Wagner Act made them the object of political struggle. In his review of the Wagner Act, Klare found:

> The indeterminancy of the text and the legislative history
> of the Act...make it clear there was no coherent or agreed-
> upon fund of ideas or principles available as a guide in
> interpreting the Act.   The statue was a texture of
> openness   and   divergency,   not   a   crystalization   of
> consensus or a signpost indicating a solitary direction for
> future developments....The Court had to select one set of
> principles and give it the imprimatur of law. This task
> was unavoidedly *a political task* (emphasis in original).[23]

According to Klare, the Wagner Act did not dispose of the basic union
demand that the law protect their right to organize and their ability to
use their market power in group conflict with employers. Rather, it was
left to political struggle to define and sharpen the contours of the law.
     Previously, voluntarism stipulated that the unions' organizational
objectives could best be achieved with the state exercising little influence
over the conduct of labor relations. Now, however, a new friendliness
exhibited by the government towards organized labor, a shift in the locus
of policy making over matters of labor policy from the courts to the
executive and legislative branches, and the organization of the unskilled
into the CIO, all combined to create a new approach to the state on the
part of unions. Unions would now attempt to secure their organizational
objectives through politics rather than outside of it. They would attempt
to secure their collective bargaining interests by trying to control and
direct labor policy, not by trying to limit its scope. While the goal
remained the same as that which had motivated unions prior to the
1930s, benefits were still to be derived through group conflict with
employers in the market, the unions' tactics were different. Perlman
describes the changes that took place in labor's approach to politics by
way of analogy:

> Prior to the airplane, it was enough to fortify a limited
> area adequately, garrison it, and confidently await the
> assault. Today, to be impregnable, a fortress must control
> an area of many hundreds of miles, even aside from the
> consideration of the wider strategy of protecting the whole
> country. The mere nuclear interest (job consciousness),
> the holding of the fortress, has thus compelled the
> erection of outlying points to keep away enemy
> bombers.[24]

The objectives remained unaltered, but the means to achieve them
required a more partisan approach than before. With their collective
bargaining rights and market power now dependent on the amount of
political influence they could demonstrate, the unions became a

permanent, if still formally independent part of the Democratic party campaign apparatus.

The politicization of labor policy that led the unions into partisan political activity took two forms. One was a shift in the institutional arena of policy making with regard to labor matters. Prior to the 1930s, Bernstein found the "courts...absorbed legislative and executive (including police) powers" in the field of labor policy.[25] Labor policy was set by the courts through their decisions. The general principle judicial decisions followed in the area of labor policy was to let "the relative economic strength of employers and employee' organizations determine policy."[26] But as a result of a groundswell of militancy and social protest by workers beginning in 1934, Congress asserted jurisdiction over the field of labor policy. This shift in the site of policy making politicized labor policy because Congress is more open to political pressure than the courts. Congress would more faithfully reflect the political balance of class forces in society because it was more open to democratic pressure. Now with the legislative branch asserting jurisdiction, labor policy would reflect the political, not economic, balance of power between labor and capital.

Secondly, the textual ambiguity of the Wagner Act and its administration and interpretation by federal appointees at the National Labor Relations Board (NLRB) also contributed to the politicization of labor policy. As we noted earlier, the Wagner Act did not prescribe any particular policy guidelines but branched off into several, sometimes conflicting, directions. It would be left to the NLRB which would reflect the prolabor or promanagement sympathies of the incumbent administration to interpret and administer the law. Like the shift in the site of policy making from the courts to Congress, the political character of the NLRB would bring labor policy in line with the relative political power held by labor and capital.

This politicization of labor policy fostered a new appreciation of electoral activity within unions. Now, for the first time, government support for their market interests was within their grasp, but only if labor could demonstrate its political strength at the polls. Perlman and Knowles write of these changes, "No longer is the politico-legislative arena a place where labor can merely pursue a mirage. It is now a real front where decisive victories can be won. Pure and simple unionism becomes a museum piece, not because of a defection from job consciousness, but because of the very fealty to job consciousness."[27]

The CIO took the lead in promoting the politicization of labor policy. Dubofsky and Van Tine write, "He [Lewis] had concluded that the future of the CIO depended on a sympathetic federal government. Without federal allies, Lewis realized organized labor could not conquer the mass production industries. His estimate of economic and political reality impelled Lewis to forge a political marriage of convenience with FDR."[28]

Once the CIO tried to enlist the state as an ally to help it obtain union recognition from employers it began to engage in partisan activity. Market ends would now be sought through social democratic means. In 1936 Lewis and Sidney Hillman formed Labor's Non-Partisan League to assist President Roosevelt's bid for reelection. The League funneled $500,000 to Democratic candidates during the campaign, far surpassing any previous political effort by organized labor. The union-party alliance began to take shape.

The CIO promoted the politicization of labor policy—and thus partisan activity—due to the nature of the constituency it sought to organize.[29] Unskilled workers lacked the economic power of skilled workers to force union recognition upon employers. But what they lacked in market power could be compensated for by their numbers in the electoral arena. Through the Non-Partisan League, Lewis sought to exchange the electoral support of CIO members for federal support of CIO organizing efforts. The League was intended to force the hand of the government on matters concerning union recognition and security, not social welfare legislation.[30]

CONCLUSION

To refer back to Perlman's metaphor: the scale of the CIO's intervention in national politics reflected an expansion of the defense perimeter surrounding the nuclear interest of the unions in collective bargaining. The politicization of labor policy wrought by the New Deal produced a reappraisal of labor's political activity. Partisan activity would have to increase. Yet, the CIO's dramatic entrance into partisan politics in the form of Labor's Non-Partisan League was intended to secure old objectives, albeit in a new way. McConnell contends:

> The break with voluntarism, then, was real and substantial. It did not, however, signify destruction of the tradition. The building and maintenance of organizational strength remained at the center of Labor's objectives. The achievement of benefits for members and for workers, in general, the ostensible justification for everything else, continued to be reserved for economic battlegrounds.[31]

Throughout the turbulent period of the CIO's schism from the AFL Lewis continued to maintain that his were not "the objectives of someone else, but the declared objectives of the AFL."[32] Lewis was not a revolutionary, but left the AFL reluctantly after failing to persuade it to accept industrial unionism. Political activity was still predicated on supporting the collective bargaining interests of the affiliated unions. But now such activity was not conceived purely in negative terms, that is, preventing the government from interfering in labor matters. Instead, the CIO promoted and supported the politicization of labor policy in order to compensate for the economic weakness of the constituency it sought to organize. Once the determination of labor policy became a political test of will between labor and management in Congress and the executive branch, the partisan activity of trade unions increased. Now that support of their collective bargaining interests depended upon their political strength the unions attached themselves to the Democratic party.

The politicization of labor policy required the unions to define the political interests of their members in broad class, as opposed to interest group terms, and to ally with the Democratic party. This became especially clear following World War II when it was management—not labor—that was able to take advantage of the changes that had occurred. The political influence of the labor movement declined in the postwar period. This was reflected in changes in labor policy: the passage of the Taft-Hartley Act, unsympathetic rulings from the NLRB, and the enactment of right-to-work laws in many states. If these setbacks were to be reversed labor needed to show greater political strength. The AFL and CIO sought to reestablish the New Deal political balance between labor and capital by forming their own political organizations. These trade union political arms were supposed to educate politically and mobilize trade union members on behalf of labor-endorsed candidates. In fact, this had the effect of drawing both the CIO and AFL into performing campaign work on behalf of the Democratic party. The union-party alliance was now essential to prevent the politicization of labor policy—which the labor movement had once viewed so favorably—from turning into a club with which to beat it.

NOTES

1. Mitchell Sviridorf, "The Responsibility of Union Officers in Politics," in *Workers as Union Members, Consumers, and as Citizens*, Bulletin No. 31, (Minneapolis: Minnesota School of Industrial Relations, 1961), 49.

2. Charles M. Rehmus, "Labor in American Politics," in William Haber, ed., *Labor in a Changing America* (New York: Basic Books, 1966), 252.

3. Norman Ware, *The Labor Movement in the United States, 1865-1890* (Gloucester, Mass.: P. Smith, 1959), 320.

4. Perlman and Taft quoted in George Higgins, *Voluntarism in Organized Labor in the United States, 1930-1940* (New York: Arno Press, 1969), 10.

5.   Louis Reed, *The Labor Philosophy of Samuel Gompers* (New York: Columbia University Press, 1930), 126-27.

6.   Ruth Horowitz, *Political Ideologies of Organized Labor: The New Deal Era* (New Brunswick, N.J.: Transaction Books, 1978), 31.

7.   Marc Karson, *American Labor and Politics, 1900-1918* (Carbondale, Ill.: Southern Illinois University Press, 1958), 130.

8.   Selig Perlman, *A Theory of the Labor Movement* (New York: MacMillan, 1928), 128.

9.   Reed, 74.

10.   Philip Taft, *The A.F. of L. in the Time of Gompers* (New York: Harper & Row, 1957), 74-75.

11.   Gary M. Fink, "The Rejection of Voluntarism," *Industrial and Labor Relations Review* 26 (January 1973): 819.

12.   Michael Paul Rogin, "Voluntarism: The Political Functions of an Antipolitical Doctrine," *Industrial and Labor Relations Review* 15 (July 1962): 521.

13.   Ibid., 527.

14.   David Brody, "Career Requirements and American Trade Unionism," in Leo Jaher, ed., *Age of Industrialism in America* (New York: Free Press, 1969): 288-304.

15.   Andrew Dawson, "The Paradox of Dynamic Technological Change and the Labour Aristocracy in the United States," *Labor History* 20 (Summer 1979): 325-52.

16.   Gwendolyn Mink, *Old Labor and New Immigrants in American Political Development* (Ithaca: Cornell University, 1986).

17.   Karson, 53.

18.   Henry Pelling, *The Origins of the Labour Party* (Oxford: Clarendon Press, 1965).

19.   Gompers is quoted in Higgins, *op. cit.*, 29.

20.   J. David Greenstone, *Labor in American Politics* 2nd ed. (Chicago: University of Chicago Press, 1977), 47.

21.   Ibid., 40-49.

22.   Melvin Dubofsky and Warren Van Tine, *John L. Lewis* (New York: Quadrangle Books, 1977), 248.

23.   Karl E. Klare, "Judicial Deradicalization of the Wagner Act and the Origins of Modern Legal Consciousness, 1937-1941," *Minnesota Law Review* 62 (March 1978): 291-92.

24.   Selig Perlman, "Labor and the New Deal in Historical Perspective," in Milton Derber and Edwin Young, eds., *Labor and the New Deal* (Madison: University of Wisconsin Press, 1957), 364.

25.   Irving Bernstein, *The Lean Years* (Boston: Houghton, Mifflin, 1960), 364.

26.   Ibid., 364.

27.   Selig Perlman and William H. Knowles, "American Unionism in the Postwar World," in T. C. T. McCormick, ed., *Problems of the Postwar World* (New York: McGraw-Hill, 1945), 40.

28.   Dubofsky, and Van Tine, 248.

29.   Horowitz *op. cit.*, 224-33; and Greenstone, *op. cit.*, 182-83 argue this position.

30.   Dubofsky and Van Tine, 249-54.

31.   Grant McConnell, *Private Power and American Democracy* (New York: Knopf, 1966), 305.

32.   David Brody, "The Expansion of the Labor Movement: Institutional Sources of Stimulus and Constraint," in David Brody, ed., *The American Labor Movement* (New York: Harper & Row, 1971), 129.

2. *From PAC to COPE*

Events conspired to reinforce the market strategy of American unions following World War II. The prosperity of the postwar years and the inhospitable political climate the unions faced made the unions' choice of strategy a logical one; indeed one that was initially very successful.

The postwar economy created conditions that were advantageous for the pursuit of benefits through the market. Between 1950 and 1969, unemployment averaged only 4.9 percent; excluding the three mild recessionary periods of 1954, 1958, and 1961, it was 4.5 percent. With the economy approaching full employment, unions were in a position to take advantage of tight labor markets in negotiations with employers.

In addition, the war created new markets at home and abroad for American goods. The war devastated European economies. These now became prime markets for American exports. At home, the release of pent-up consumer demand from the war also created new market opportunities for American business. Factories ran at full capacity to meet the increased demand. Between 1956 and 1969, overtime averaged three hours per worker in manufacturing. Union cooperation in production was essential if business was to take advantage of the opportunities for expansion and profit that lay before it.

Profits were available to purchase such cooperation. Between 1947 and 1969 net profits after taxes in all manufacturing industries except newspapers rose 135 percent. Between 1955 and 1969, after tax profits tripled in primary metal industries, and increased 160 percent in motor vehicles and 198 percent in electrical machinery and equipment.[1] The profits that American industry accumulated served as a fund from which increased wages and benefits for workers could be drawn and the demands of the unions' market strategy satisfied.

On the political side, the environment that unions encountered at the end of World War II was as grim as economic conditions were favorable. The political program of the unions was stymied. Moreover, conservatives sought to reverse the organizational gains unions had made during the 1930s via the same legislative path unions had used to achieve them. The guns were being turned against the fort. Clegg writes, "Following the New Deal, American unions soon came to rely heavily on the support of the law. This dependence provided an opening to later legislatures who believed that collective bargaining and trade unionism needed to be curbed rather than encouraged."[2]

The shift in the political fortunes of organized labor following World War II was manifested in two ways. First, the CIO's postwar social program to complete the New Deal was rejected by Congress. Finding its proposals for welfare state measures checked in Congress, it took them to the negotiating table as items to be included in collective bargaining. Secondly, unions found their organizational rights under attack. Both were important in keeping the unions within the bounds of a market strategy.

POLITICAL DEFEAT

At the end of World War II, the CIO presented its reconversion program to Congress. This program sought to restore the momentum of the New Deal which the war had temporarily interrupted. The cool reception the CIO's program received in Congress was convincing evidence that the war did not mark a temporary hiatus of the New Deal but its end. Efforts to have the minimum wage raised to $0.65 were disappointingly compromised at $0.55. A bid for supplementary unemployment insurance never got past the House Ways and Means Committee and, finally, The Murray-Wagner Full Employment Act was "amended beyond recognition."[3] In 1948 the CIO again hoped that Congress would complete the aborted work of the New Deal. It submitted proposals to Congress for national health insurance, increases in social security coverage and benefits, and a national unemployment insurance program. Again its proposals suffered defeat in a Congress dominated by a conservative coalition of Republicans and Southern Democrats.

With its social program defeated in Congress, the CIO redirected its efforts. The same proposals that it submitted to Congress it now brought to the negotiating table with management. CIO unions proposed that health insurance and pension provisions be included in collective bargaining agreements. Previously, collective bargaining had been largely concerned with issues of union recognition, wages, and hours. Now wage supplements became a major item in negotiations.[4] The unions sought to receive from the market what they had been disappointed in achieving through legislation. Between 1948 and 1959, the number of workers covered by health insurance and pension plans under collective bargaining tripled. Private welfare expenditures increased from one percent of total employer compensation costs in 1940 to eight percent by 1972.[5] The ability of industry to absorb these costs and the inability of the CIO to get its social program through Congress conspired to make the CIO an innovator in collective bargaining. Social insurance was to be achieved through the market not legislation.

The second political issue in which the fortunes of organized labor suffered a reversal was in the field of labor legislation. The economy was able to absorb the defeat of the CIO's social program, but the legislative attack on the organizing and collective bargaining interests of trade unions that commenced with the end of the war struck at the vitals of trade unionism.

The legislative backlash against labor began during World War II. The 1942 elections were a disaster for the CIO. James Carey, president of the International Union of Electrical Workers, estimated that the CIO lost 42 prolabor congressmen from the House. Worried by this election defeat, CIO President Philip Murray commissioned Nathan Cowan, the CIO's congressional lobbyist, J. Raymond Walsh, head of the CIO's research department, and John Brophy, director of CIO state councils, to write a position paper that considered alternatives open to the CIO. The Cowan-Brophy-Walsh Report emphasized "the need to operate inside the Democratic Party."[6] It recommended that the CIO set up an autonomous political organization to assist the Democratic party in campaign work.

It did not take long for Congress to act in ways the CIO feared. In 1943 Congress passed the Smith-Connally Act over a Presidential veto. This bill required a 30 day cooling-off period in the case of strikes, an NLRB administered strike vote before work stoppages could occur in noncritical industries, and it empowered the President to seize plants and industries in which strikes threatened the war effort. The bill was a serious setback for labor because its original intent was simply to prevent wartime stoppages in coal production. But sentiment for legislation that would suspend coal strikes for the duration of the war had been converted into a general attack upon the entire labor movement.

In response to passage of the bill, the CIO rushed to implement the recommendations of the Cowan-Brophy-Walsh Report. Gall writes, "More than anything else, the CIO leadership's interest in building a political machine at the national, state and local levels stemmed from fear of legislative attacks."[7] In 1943, the CIO created the Political Action Committee (PAC) to repel further legislative assaults upon the autonomy of trade unions. PAC would politically educate the membership, raise money, and organize register-and-vote drives in support of PAC-endorsed candidates. Significantly, PAC also had a minorities department to organize register-and-vote drives among blacks outside the CIO membership.

The midterm elections of 1946 returned a Republican majority to both the House and the Senate. As part of their effort to curb the rights of unions, conservatives first tried to pressure the Civil Service Commission to purge the NLRB of two-thirds of its hearing examiners. According to Senator Alexander Wiley (R-Wisconsin), the hearing officers presently employed were "inimical to the welfare of the private enterprise" and showed favoritism in their decisions to organized labor.[8] Liberals in Congress foiled this ploy. But in 1947 Congress passed the Labor-Management Relations Act (LMRA), popularly known as the Taft-Hartley Act. Union leaders heatedly denounced the bill as unfair, punitive, and restrictive. Among its provisions, the bill outlawed the closed shop, jurisdictional strikes, and secondary boycotts.

The passage of Taft-Hartley awakened the political resolve of the AFL. During the 1930s, the AFL responded to the politicization of labor relations without enthusiasm. The AFL tried to subvert the Fair Labor Standards Act while it was pending in Congress and supported it only retroactive to its passage.[9] When the Wagner Act was passed the AFL joined a noisy chorus that demanded basic changes in the law. Only when an avalanche of proposed amendments to the Act threatened to turn it into an antiunion instrument did the AFL defend it. But the passage of Taft-Hartley in 1947 steered the AFL onto a course already traveled by the CIO. In 1947 the AFL created Labor's League for Political Education (LLPE). The League was to carry out functions identical to those of CIO-PAC. According to then AFL Secretary-Treasurer George Meany, the membership had to be made "politically conscious; develop their politics in their own self-interest, not for the purpose of running the country, but for the purpose of protecting ourselves."[10]

The ability to direct legislation affecting their organizational interests upon which they had staked their abandonment of voluntarist tactics was eluding the unions. McConnell writes, "In the period after World War II, it could be reasonably argued that the government was more likely to hamper than to assist the exercise of union power."[11] In response to the legislative backlash against organized labor, the CIO created PAC and the AFL formed LLPE. In an article published in 1958, LLPE Director and later COPE Director James McDevitt admitted, "The simple fact is that it was the Smith-Connally Act of 1943 and its successor in Taft-Hartley in 1947 that compelled the present day labor movement to enter into politics. Were it not for these two pieces of punitive legislation it is possible that we would not be expending the effort we are in the political field."[12]

Through the establishment of PAC and LLPE the unions became more closely allied with the Democratic party. This was true of PAC from the start and was an explicit purpose of the organization as stated in the Cowan-Brophy-Walsh Report. LLPE was more timid in its partisanship, but in 1952 the AFL endorsed Adlai Stevenson, the Democratic party nominee for President.[13]

In 1950 PAC led a heavily publicized but unsuccessful campaign to defeat Senator Robert Taft who had guided LMRA through the Senate.

McConnell concludes that by 1952, when Dwight D. Eisenhower was elected President and the Republicans controlled both houses of Congress that, "The efforts of Labor's leadership to share in the exercise of public authority had failed."[14] Perhaps only the merger of the AFL and CIO could restore labor's political influence which was so essential now that labor policy had been politicized.

THE URGE TO MERGE

McConnell argues that the 1952 elections were politically a "great turning point. Henceforth, union leaders could not be sanguine about their prospects as collaborators in the work of government at any high level."[15] The new strategy upon which the unions had embarked beginning with the Depression, to go through politics to achieve their organizational objectives rather than outside it, was threatening the very results they hoped to achieve. Labor had altered its appreciation of politics when it was at the height of its political influence. But political tides shift. Labor now discovered in the 1950s that the consequences of the New Deal were not necessarily favorable. Instead, the politicization of labor relations introduced by the New Deal would benefit whichever side could swing the bigger club. The effect of the New Deal upon union security was an open one, contingent upon the competing class capacities of political actors. Now with officials at the helm less friendly to labor than either the Roosevelt or Truman administrations had been, the politicization of labor policy introduced by the New Deal—even the very agencies created by the New Deal—became the opening through which the Republicans launched a political attack against union security. The same institutional machinery which had sustained labor under Roosevelt was now being used to restrain it.

The results of the 1952 election presaged a new political offensive against organized labor. Although the CIO and the AFL both supported the Democrats, the election was a solid Republican victory. As labor surveyed the wreckage, it found it could count on only 140, or about one-third of the votes in the House. This was a steep drop from the 209 votes it mustered in 1950 to block amendments that would have stiffened the Taft-Hartley Act. Few of these congressmen were influential, none was a committee chairman, and only 10 of the 26 members of the House Education and Labor Committee were considered friendly to unions. The view from the Senate was a bit brighter. Although only 7 out of 21 CIO-endorsed Senatorial candidates won, dependables such as Paul Douglas (D-Illinois), Herbert Lehman (D-New York), and Lister Hill (D-Alabama) remained on the Senate Labor Committee. The Committee's chairmanship passed from James Murray (D-Montana) to Robert Taft's personal selection, H. Alexander Smith (R-New Jersey). Taft became Majority Leader. Ideologically, Reichard notes that "the overall tenor of Republicanism in the Eighty-third Congress was undeniably nationalist and conservative."[16]   Except for foreign policy, President Eisenhower shared and reaffirmed the orthodox and traditional Republican sentiments of Congress.

But the election results reflected deeper, more serious problems that beset organized labor. *Business Week* wrote, "The outcome of the 1952 election has the effect not of initiating a new trend but of accelerating something in motion."[17]   McCarthyism and the terms on which the public debate were being conducted paralyzed the labor movement. The identity between staunch anticommunist feelings and attacks on the New Deal which McCarthy and his supporters were able to establish forced labor to prove its patriotism by repudiating its political program.   An attempt to defend that program was seen as evidence of subversion. Concerning Senator John Butler's proposals to amend the Internal Security Act in 1953, David Oshinsky writes, "These provisions were viewed by liberals as a blatant attempt to rid the labor movement of its more aggressive leadership by putting labor leaders in such a position that a strong stand on any controversial social, economic or political issue could easily be interpreted as subversive."[18]   The Army-McCarthy hearings occurred in the midst of negotiations over the No-Raiding agreement, a key document in merger negotiations.

Under the camouflage of McCarthyism and now equipped with the authority of Congress and the President, conservatives trained their guns on organized labor. The assault on the organizational rights of unions was conducted on three fronts: in Congress by the effort to revise the Taft-Hartley Act; in the executive branch by the appointment of an unsympathetic NLRB; and in the states by the passage of restrictive labor legislation.   Each will be discussed in turn.   As the political threat migrated and intensified from one arena to the next, the urgency for unity within organized labor increased.   Finally, the challenge loomed so large that the AFL and CIO agreed to merge even though the issues over which they continued to disagree remained unresolved. The urgency for unity came from the state. Organized labor thought it saw in merger a way to pool its resources against political attack and simultaneously rebuild the New Deal coalition to reclaim political influence.

In January 1953, CIO President Walter Reuther and AFL President George Meany met in Washington and agreed to revive the Joint AFL-CIO Unity Committee which had last met during the Korean War. A follow-up meeting was scheduled for February but due to the untimely death of CIO Executive Vice-President Allen Heywood it was postponed to April 17.   In March at the Auto Workers convention, Reuther stipulated three principles to be upheld in merger negotiations: that basic union structures remain intact; that machinery be established to resolve jurisdictional disputes; and that the AFL eliminate all unions that practice racial discrimination or racketeering.[19] The April meeting of the two presidents was strained because Meany resented that Reuther was setting conditions to merger even before negotiations had begun.   It was resolved, however, that two specific areas of contention be studied by a subcommittee: the raiding of union membership and the problem of overlapping jurisdictions. *U.S. News and World Report* predicted confidently that "merger talk is once again bringing leaders of the CIO and AFL together. But as in the past, such talk is almost sure to end in disagreement."[20]

Progress was also slow because the AFL was initially wooed by the new Administration. It enjoyed a prestige and influence in Washington under the Republicans it had never enjoyed under the Democrats, and it replaced the CIO as labor's spokesman in the nation's capital. Eisenhower chose Martin Durkin from the Plumbers Union as his secretary of labor, and Lloyd Mashburn from the Los Angeles Building and Construction Trades Council was selected his undersecretary of labor. In January 1953, Taft submitted 16 amendments to the Taft-Hartley Act. Two of his amendments were aimed specifically at mollifying AFL objections to the law. One proposal would have given de-facto recognition to the closed shop in the building trades, and another would have eased secondary boycott restrictions. The AFL, therefore, felt no urgency to proceed with the merger because the Republicans appeared anxious to satisfy their particular demands in the area of labor policy. The CIO on the other hand, complained that Taft's revisions showed "discrimination in favor of particular unions."[21] John L. Lewis accused Meany and Richard Gray, director of the Building and Construction Trades Department of the AFL, of holding clandestine meetings with the Administration to gain exemptions for the building trades from Taft-Hartley provisions.

However, the romance between the new Administration and the AFL did not last past September. The more the two parties met in the course of the Taft-Hartley controversy of 1953, the less they came to care for each other until finally, Durkin resigned. The battle over Taft-Hartley revisions ended the AFL 's short honeymoon with the Republicans.

From the moment he took office, Durkin found the going tough within the Eisenhower administration. The President pledged to build up the Department of Labor, but Durkin found his budget slashed by 14 percent. His appointments to fill assistant secretary positions were not approved. Leo Werts was vetoed by his home-state senator, John Butler, and John Edelmen's name never made it past the White House. Durkin refused to fill a third position, expected to go to management, until a CIO man was placed in his department. In July, six months after his appointment, the three positions were still vacant. Finally, in a cabinet which contained "eight millionaires and a plumber" it was common knowledge that Durkin was an outsider.

Durkin could withstand these disparagements because he was intent on revising Taft-Hartley. A tripartite commission that Durkin assigned to prepare legislative recommendations on Taft-Hartley for Congress was sabotaged by its management representatives. Durkin then submitted Taft-Hartley revisions to the White House based upon studies by the Department of Labor. Meetings designed to reach agreement on revisions within the Administration proved fruitless. In mid-March the Administration announced that it would not have a bill ready until after Congress held hearings.

The testimony of labor representatives at Senate and House hearings on Taft-Hartley revisions was contradictory, petty, and uncoordinated. Disagreement over how the Act should be modified appeared among the United Mine Workers, the CIO, the AFL, and even within the AFL. Demands varied from Lewis' proposal to return to voluntarism and repeal all labor laws including the Wagner Act to suggestions by particular unions for narrow and specialized changes to suit their specific needs.[22] By April, *Business Week* reported "The amendments to the Taft-Hartley Act that are getting the most serious consideration are those prepared not by labor, but by industry. Behind this is an unusually rigorous campaign that has focused attention on proposals to make the law more stringent...Union spokesmen are clearly on the defensive."[23]

In May, H. Alexander Smith, Senate Labor Committee Chairman, released a working paper that contained 36 changes in the Act. Labor leaders were stunned. It contained some provisions which had not had enough strength to even reach the stage of a vote in the Eightieth Congress. Some of Smith's proposals would permit states to regulate strikes and picketing regardless of whether interstate commerce was involved, would empower states to "protect the health or safety" of the people in labor disputes, and would eliminate all small businesses from the area of interstate commerce and thus the protection of the NLRB. The Administration had still not submitted its proposals.

Negotiations between the Department of Labor and the White House resumed following the hearings. Whether the department and the Administration ever reached an agreement is still a matter of controversy.

Revisions proposed by the White House were to have been sent to Congress on July 31, but Senator Taft died on that day. In deference to his passing away a decision was made to temporarily withhold the revisions. Congress adjourned shortly thereafter. On August 3, the *Wall Street Journal* published a leaked copy of the proposals, all generally favorable to labor. The outcry from business leaders was loud and vociferous. Durkin appealed to the White House to release and endorse the proposals to counter the opposition campaign. The White House demurred. Durkin maintained that the revisions were the Administration's final position on the issue and that all 19 amendments had the approval of the president. The White House flatly denied this and claimed that the proposals were only a working paper.[24] On August 19, Durkin met with Eisenhower and discussions with the White House staff resumed. In those discussions Durkin refused to compromise and insisted that the agreement on the 19 points be honored. The White House staff stood equally firm. Blocked in gaining favorable revisions of

Taft-Hartley and feeling betrayed, Durkin submitted his resignation on August 31.

The AFL convention in September took place in a heated and antagonistic atmosphere following Durkin's resignation. Vice-President Richard Nixon appeared before the convention and was greeted with derision when he termed Durkin's resignation the result of a "misunderstanding". Meany fully supported Durkin's action and said it put the AFL's relationship with the Administration in its proper perspective. He also used Durkin's resignation as an opportunity to call for more political action by the affiliates. Jim McDevitt, director of LLPE, reminded delegates that "We are in politics for a very simple reason—to protect our members legislatively."[25]

The vigor of the business offensive on Taft-Hartley revisions and the corresponding disunity of labor did not escape the notice of the delegates. A. Philip Randolph, president of the Brotherhood of Sleeping Car Porters, submitted a resolution calling for labor unity claiming that schism is "largely responsible for anti-labor legislation and that without the healing of this split no basic amendments to the Taft-Hartley Act favorable to the wage earner will be made."[26]

In 1954 the Administration finally submitted its amendments and the Senate Labor Committee reported them out of Committee intact. The revisions were far less liberal than those on which Durkin thought he had reached an agreement with the Administration last July 1953. Fearing harmful amendments from the Senate floor and uncertain whether they could defeat them, labor supporters resorted to parliamentary tactics to have the bill recommitted which effectively killed it.

The contest over Taft-Hartley revisions began with organized labor, particularly the AFL, cautiously optimistic of gaining favorable changes in the Act. At the end they were lucky to emerge with a stalemate, feeling fortunate that the Act was not made more restrictive.

While the Taft-Hartley controversy raged, the subcommittee of the Joint Unity Committee charged with investigating the problem of raiding and overlapping jurisdictions met. On May 4, 1953, it released figures on raiding supplied to it by the NLRB for the years 1951 and 1952. The NLRB's records showed 1,245 cases of raiding but a net transfer of only 8,000 members. The subcommittee concluded that raiding was widespread, costly, and its net result was negligible.

A no-raiding agreement was prepared. Arthur Goldberg, then General Council of the CIO and involved in the unity negotiations, maintains that "The draft prepared was a strong one designed to provide a firm, binding, and enforceable contract which would effectively stop raiding."[27] This is inaccurate and misleading on two counts.

First, the agreement only preserved the existing representational claims of unions at *status quo ante*. This applied only to unions that signed the agreement, which left the raiding of those who did not sign a legitimate activity. The agreement did provide some machinery to arbitrate disputes, but unions were under no compulsion to abide by the referee's decision. It did not touch on disputes over the unorganized but only applied to those workers already under contract. Furthermore, it did not begin to untangle the thicket of disputes that arose from overlapping jurisdictional lines—one of its original purposes—or from the craft raiding of departmental units within industrial plants. Finally, unions did not rush to comply with it. The Steelworkers signed late and the Teamsters, by far the worst pirate of other union's members and a special concern of CIO unions, never did. The original agreement was supposed to go into effect on January 1, 1954, but by that date only the names of the two federation presidents and their secretary-treasurers appeared on the document. By June 9, 1954, however, the No-Raiding Agreement was signed by 29 out of 32 CIO affiliates and 65 out of 110 AFL unions.

Goldberg's optimistic assessment of the agreement was also insensitive to the political advantages that Meany and Reuther saw in it. Not only was raiding bad publicity, but it diverted the resources and attention of the labor movement from political action into internecine strife. In fact, it was only by emphasizing its political advantages that Meany was able to convince a skeptical and reluctant Executive Council to accept the agreement.[28] At the ceremony to celebrate the signing of the agreement Meany warned, "Labor in America can no longer afford to be divided. We cannot waste our strength and substance in civil war while the enemies of human progress step up their attack on us in the economic, political and legislative fronts."[29]

The first session of the Eighty-third Congress ended without any legislative action on the Taft-Hartley Act. Yet, even before that political front had closed, the Administration launched a second offensive against labor through the NLRB. Eisenhower's appointments to the NLRB drastically altered the Board's political complexion. The new Board proceeded to modify substantially the way the National Labor Relations Act was administered and interpreted. It moved quickly to transform the stalemate labor had been fortunate to save on Taft-Hartley revisions into a defeat. Labor was able to prevent the law from changing in form only to find that it was changing in practice.

On June 30, 1953, Chairman Paul Herzog, a Truman appointee recommended by Senator Robert Wagner, resigned. He was replaced by Guy Farmer who immediately alarmed labor leaders by his record of dissents against unions in his first month on the Board. At his inauguration, Farmer spoke of the need to decentralize labor relations and provide a greater role for the states in making labor policy. Both the AFL and CIO vehemently opposed this proposal.

The term of John Houston expired in August, and he was replaced on Taft's recommendation by Philip Ray Rodgers. A memo circulating in the White House at the time indicated that with the appointment of Farmer and Rodgers "a start" in "curing the N.L.R.B." had been made.[30]

A third Board vacancy appeared in September. It was not until March 1954 that this seat was filled by Albert C. Beeson. Beeson could boast 14 years of exclusive representation of management interests. No previous Board appointee was ever chosen directly from the ranks of management (or labor). Prior to his appointment he served seven years as director of Industrial Relations at Food Machinery and Chemical Corporation in San Jose, California. In those seven years his firm suffered three serious strikes. At his Senate confirmation hearings, the CIO expressed opposition to his appointment. John L. Lewis referred to Beeson as a union buster and protested his appointment. Then in Beeson's own testimony a possible conflict of interest was revealed. He was approved in the Senate by a vote of 45-42.

Prior to Beeson's appointment the Board had been split 2-2 in over 20 cases. Beeson's tie-breaking vote made possible the reversal of many of the Board's former decisions. The new Eisenhower Board overturned so many prior Board decisions that it earned the nickname the National Labor Reversal Board. Even the *National Association of Manufacturers Law Digest* had to admit: "They [NLRB] seem to have proceeded on the assumption that since they were appointed by a new Administration they had a license to overhaul any or all of the Board's policies. They have proceeded to imbue the Board with the employer-oriented interests of the new Administration."[31]

Through its decisions the NLRB, in effect, amended NLRA in a manner that antilabor forces in Congress had originally proposed but failed to pass. Looking at the Board's decisions as a whole, law professor, W. Willard Wirtz noted how solicitous and responsive to the concerns of employers they were. He writes:

> The new Board has restored board license to employers who choose to oppose, in various ways, union organizing activities....The new law of employer persuasion traces directly to the national election of 1952 and to the subsequent appointment of a majority more responsive to the sentiments or experiences of employers. It can hardly be questioned that the one most reliable factor in predicting what the Board will do...is its apparent subscription...to the prevailing management point of view.[32]

The NLRB is an example of an agency created by the New Deal which labor initially viewed favorably, but one which it discovered in the 1950s shifted with political winds. The following figures in table 2.1 reveal how much the NLRB reflected the conservative bias of the Administration.[33]

TABLE 2-1: UNFAIR LABOR PRACTICE CHARGES FILED WITH THE
NLRB, 1952-1956

	1952	1953	1954	1955	1956
Total Number of Charges Filed	5454	5469	5965	6171	5265
Against Unions	1148 (21%)	1060 (19%)	1542 (27%)	1809 (29%)	1743 (33%)
Against Employers	4306 (79%)	4409 (81%)	4373 (73%)	4362 (71%)	3522 (67%)
Total Number of Complaints	699	950	821	497	713
Against Unions	118 (17%)	193 (20%)	230 (28%)	210 (42%)	325 (51%)
Against Employers	581 (83%)	757 (80%)	591 (72%)	287 (58%)	314 (49%)

*This does not include 74 complaints by Southern Bell against the
Communications Workers of America.

In 1952 five times more unfair labor practice charges were filed
with the Board against employers than against unions. This five-to-one
ratio closely corresponds to the ratio of complaints between employers
and unions that the Board eventually prosecuted in 1952. By 1956,
however, after Eisenhower had revamped the Board, the ratio of charges
to complaints was no longer in tandem. In 1956, even though three
times more unfair labor practice charges against employers were filed
with the Board than against unions, the Board chose to review more
unfair labor practice charges against unions than against employers.
This acted as a signal to different groups to avail themselves of the
Board's services. In 1956 unions submitted 31 percent fewer unfair
labor practice charges to the Board than they did in 1952. In that same
four-year period, charges from employers almost doubled. As a result,
the number of grievances filed against unions rose 52 percent in this
period, while those filed against employers declined by 18 percent. The
whole complexion of the Board had shifted toward employers under the
Republicans; from the beginning of the process and the filing of an

unfair labor practice charge to the kind of decisions emanating from the Board. This political reversal of the NLRB corresponded to the new political balance of power struck between labor and capital in the Eisenhower years.

The Eisenhower Board was the object of continual attack and calumny at AFL and CIO conventions. When Alex Rose, president of the Hatters Union, offered a unity resolution at the 1954 A.F.L. convention because "it would provide labor with the strongest weapon it could forge for the protection of its economic position," he cited "the stacking of the NLRB against labor" as evidence of the general conservative trend.[34]

Following a stalemate in Congress on Taft-Hartley—only to have the Act substantially rewritten by the NLRB—another front opened up that labor had to defend. In 1953, Alabama, the stronghold of organized labor in the South, passed a right-to-work law. In 1954 South Carolina, Louisiana, and Mississippi followed suit. The state legislature of Kansas passed a right-to-work law only to have it vetoed by the governor. In all, 19 state legislatures considered such legislation in 1954 to 1955 and it reached the stage of a vote in five states. By 1955 Utah could be added to the list of right-to-work states. Between 1949 and 1952 only one state had adopted a right-to-work law. Within 18 months, from 1953 to 1955, 5 states had passed such legislation.

The shift in the NLRB's sympathies and a new wave of antilabor legislation that emanated from the states were the primary concern of labor leaders in 1954. A. H. Raskin of the *New York Times* reported, "the advent of Labor Day finds organized labor intent on political battles rather than in jousts with the employers on the picket line."[35] At the annual AFL convention *Business Week* noted, "the political theme was almost an obsession."[36] At the CIO convention, president of the Steelworkers, David McDonald offered a labor unity resolution maintaining it was necessary to bolster labor's political strength. Later, John C. Schulter, a delegate from the Retail, Wholesale, and Department Store Workers rose to support a unity resolution and describe what he felt was "the paramount issue facing the entire labor movement":

> I have been with the CIO since there has been a CIO....I am no Johnny-come-lately. The last 16 of those 18 years have been spent below the Mason-Dixon line, so I think I have a pretty good evaluation of the situation....
>
> I feel that the entire labor movement in this country is facing a crisis at this moment. There have been three significant developments, all of which may alter the complexion not only of the CIO but the AFL....
>
> We are faced at the moment with the possibility of a recession....Second, since 1947, with the Taft-Hartley Act, the labor movement including the AFL and other unions, has been on the defensive. Third, especially below the Mason-Dixon line there has been an anti-labor

movement that today finds 10 out of 14 Southern states with laws that bar both the union shop and the maintenance of membership....If this is a general trend we are in trouble.

There is an axiom in the labor movement that when you are in trouble, you look for partners.[37]

The conventions of affiliated unions were also occupied with resolutions and speeches that offered labor unity as a means the unions might use to augment its political defenses. *Business Week* reported, "Conventions agreed that unity is essential—perhaps to a greater degree than ever before—because of growing state legislation regulating unions, the tighter economy, and the necessity of presenting a united front against the Republican Administration." But it placated its readers and confidently predicted that unity was still "far off" and, if in the offing, "won't be done quickly."[38] It cited jurisdictional and representational disputes as the reasons why unity still lay in the distant future. Within four months the AFL and CIO agreed to merge.

Business Week made such a poor prediction because it believed that jurisdictional disputes would have to be resolved before merger could take place. And it knew how hard it would be for the federations to reach agreement on that issue.[39] Meany and Reuther knew it as well. The Joint Unity Committee met in Washington, D.C. on October 15, 1954. Reuther repeated the conditions he had mentioned more than a year ago under which he would consider merger. The AFL did not dissent but Meany stated impatiently, "We can go after unity the long way or the short way. The long way is to solve all our problems before merging."[40] The CIO members agreed to go after unity the "short way".

This decision was the crucial break in merger negotiations. What Meany was offering was to merge first and settle problems of dual jurisdictions later. Rather than solved, jurisdictional disputes would now be brought within the united federation.[41] Meany decided to forego haggling over each point because, as he told Goulden, "We wouldn't live long enough to do it by that method."[42] Given the political setbacks labor had received, with the end of the decline nowhere in sight, labor leaders could not afford to wait. Merger was imperative.

The merger still had to be ratified at separate conventions of the AFL and CIO. The AFL met first in New York. In the convention's opening address, Meany spoke bluntly about labor's precarious political position, "I will tell you frankly that in the last seven or eight years we have not measured our legislative achievement on the basis of forward progress, but on the reverse basis of how much or how little we have been hurt by a session of the legislature."[43] Later at the convention, a resolution on labor unity offered by the Brotherhood of Painters spoke of Taft-Hartley, right-to-work laws, and the general legislative attack on labor as making labor unity imperative.[44] AFL Secretary-Treasurer William Schnitzler presented the Executive Council's report on merger to the delegates. He emphasized that the council was well aware that the newly proposed constitution was "not a perfect document" and might later need revision, but it still deserved their assent.[45] It was approved unanimously. After some debate on the unity resolution at the CIO convention, the delegates approved merger by a vote of 5,712,000 to 120,000. Union was now consummated.

Some analysts argue that a "convergence theory" between the AFL and CIO best explains the merger. They argue that as the AFL accepted industrial unionism and revived its organizing militancy and the CIO became more bureaucratic and conservative, there was little to differentiate the two organizations. John Hutchinson writes, "With a growing identity of character there came an increased interest in cooperation....The merger convention only ratified...a union which had already taken place."[46] But Wilson argues that it is precisely in cases where organizations share overlapping goals and jurisdictions that merger is most difficult. It is only under the threat of crisis and imminent disaster that the leaders of organizations that share a common domain can be moved to join forces.[47] The convergence theory also overlooks how much the final agreement was a "marriage of diplomacy, not one of love."[48] It neglects the fact that the merger bypassed and left unresolved crucial jurisdictional issues that had separated the two organizations. Finally, this perspective cannot explain why merger took place in 1955 because it does not make reference to the pressure of political events the labor movement faced: legislative challenges in Congress, the appointment of an unsympathetic NLRB, and the passage of restrictive labor laws at the state level.

Both Meany and Reuther thought of merger in relation to the deteriorating political climate. They hoped that by consolidating the two organizations they would be able to check and reverse this trend. The political dividends they hoped to collect from merger were more money for political work, greater influence within the Democratic party, more pressure on antilabor candidates, and greater organizational efficiency. Meany appeared at a National Urban League luncheon in Milwaukee in September 1955 and said, "We are going to get into the halls of Congress and the state legislatures people who will listen sympathetically....This is the key to the passage of liberal legislation. Under the merger we will forge the key."[49]

Meany and Reuther were not alone. Contemporaries also viewed the merger in decidedly political terms. At a Presidential news conference John Herling asked President Eisenhower if he felt the merger might create the danger of a labor monopoly. The President misinterpreted the question believing it to refer to whether he thought labor might monopolize votes, not industrial actions.[50] Business spokesmen were also attracted to the political consequences of the merger. Harold Stassen called the merger "politically dangerous" before the Economic Club of Detroit.[51] The president of the National Association of Manufacturers, Henry Riter, termed the merger a "manifestation of lust for power on the part of labor leaders."[52] The *New York Times* editorialized, "The probable effects of the proposed merger makes interesting speculation. Strangely enough the most obvious one has no defined roots in the text of the merger agreement: a stronger and more aggressive role in the nation's political life."[53]

When the AFL and CIO merged, both Federations combined their respective political organizations, LLPE and PAC, to form COPE. COPE was to perform the same tasks as its progenitors: educate the members to the policy positions of the unions, register voters, and mobilize support for labor-endorsed candidates. Labor leaders hoped that the newly merged organization would prove stronger than its component parts.

CONCLUSION

COPE's origins lay in the concerted attack upon the organizational rights of trade unions that took place during Eisenhower's first term. Labor leaders took these threats so seriously that they were willing to merge even though crucial jurisdictional differences remained unresolved.[54] The politicization of labor policy which labor had once been able to manipulate to its advantage had been captured by business. COPE's job was to once again make labor policy a servant of the trade unions.

Once management began to gain the political advantage in determining labor policy, the unions could not afford to take a haphazard approach to political organization. The new terrain upon which policy affecting their relations with management was being contested demanded sustained and deliberate political organization.

The merger of PAC and LLPE was supposed to make COPE a more effective and efficient organization than either one of them had been individually. But as the review of COPE's structure in the next chapter reveals, the decentralization of authority and resources within the AFL-CIO—mandated by the market strategy the American labor movement follows—severely limits COPE's effectiveness. Without authority to coerce the internationals and their local unions, and without the means to reach beyond them to mobilize the membership, COPE resembles a "rope of sand". Due, in part, to the AFL-CIO's decentralized structure, the political dividends that merger was supposed to bring never materialized.

NOTES

1. Federal Trade Commission, *Quarterly Financial Reports* (Washington, D.C.: U.S. Government Printing Office, 1947-69).

2. Hugh Clegg, *Trade Unionism Under Collective Bargaining: A Theory Based on Comparison of Six Countries* (Oxford: B. Blackwell, 1976), 111.

3. James C. Foster, *The Union Politic: The C.I.O. Political Action Committee* (Columbia: University of Missouri Press, 1975), 51.

4. Stanley Aronowitz, *False Promises: The Shaping of American Working Class Consciousness* (New York: McGraw Hill, 1973), 364-67.

5. U.S. Bureau of Labor Statistics, "Measures of Compensation, 1972," Bulletin 1941, (Washington, D.C.: Department of Labor, 1972).

6. Foster, 9

7. Gilbert Gall, "Sterile Combat: Labor, Politics, and Right-to-Work," (Ph.D., Wayne State University, 1984), 47.

8. Ralph Fuchs, "The Hearing Examiner Fiasco under the Administrative Procedures Act," *Harvard Law Review* 63 (March 1950): 743.

9. Ruth Horowitz, *Political Ideologies of Organized Labor: The New Deal Era* (New Brunswick, N.J.: Transaction Books, 1978).

10. Meany is quoted in Philip Taft, *The A.F. of L. From the Death of Gompers to the Merger* (New York: Harper & Row, 1959), 313.

11. Grant McConnell, *Private Power and American Democracy* (New York: Knopf, 1966), 316.

12. Jim McDevitt, "The People Are Deeply Concerned," *The American Federationist* 65 (August 1958): 11.

13. See the discussion of this endorsement in the AFL Convention Proceedings, 1952, 74.

14. McConnell, 316.

15. Ibid., 313.

16. Gary Reichard, *The Reaffirmation of Republicanism* (Knoxville: University of Tennessee Press, 1975), 48.

17. "Labor's Problems: Laws and Leaders," *Business Week* (Nov. 15, 1952): 155.

18.   David Oshinsky, *Senator Joseph McCarthy and the American Labor Movement* (Columbia: University of Missouri Press, 1976), 178.

19.   United Automobile, Aerospace and Agricultural Implements Workers of America Convention Proceedings, 1953, 47.

20.   "Union Warfare on the Horizon," *U.S. News and World Report* (April 10, 1953): 88.

21.   *Wall Street Journal,* (February 9, 1953).

22.   U.S. Senate Committee on Labor and Public Welfare, *Hearings on Taft-Hartley Revisions,* 83rd Cong., 1st sess., 613-16 and 1648-57.

23.   "Industry Speaks Up," *Business Week* (April 18, 1953): 179.

24.   For a description of this controversy, see Gerald Pomper, "Labor Legislation: The Revision of Taft-Hartley in 1953-1954." *Labor History* 6 (Spring 1965): 143-59; Gerald Pomper, "Organized Labor in Politics: The Campaign to Revise the Taft-Hartley Act," (Ph.d., Princeton University, 1959); and Gilbert Gall, *op. cit.,* 83-96.

25.   AFL Convention Proceedings, 1953, 565.

26.   Ibid., 412.

27.   Arthur Goldberg, *Labor United* (New York: McGraw-Hill, 1956), 77.

28.   Joseph Goulden, *Meany* (New York: Atheneum, 1972), 197.

29.   AFL Convention Proceedings, 1954, 57.

30.   Seymour   Scher,   "Regulatory   Agency   Control   Through Appointment: The Case of the Eisenhower Administration," *The Journal of Politics* 23 (November 1961): 672.

31.   Quoted in Scher, 687.

32.   W. Willard Wirtz, "The New NLRB: Herein of Employer Persuasion," *Northwestern Law Review* 49 (1955): 611.

33.   Figures are compiled from the *Annual Report of the NLRB* for 1953-57.

34.   AFL Convention Proceedings, 1954, 404.

35.   *New York Times* (September 9, 1954).

36.   "Labor Is Seeing Democratic," *Business Week* (October 2, 1954): 150.

37.   CIO Convention Proceedings, 1954, 354.

38.   "Labor is Seeing Democratic," *Business Week* (October 2, 1954): 158.

39.   See also *Engineering News-Record* (May 3, 1956): 112 for a similar view.

40.   Goulden, 200.

41.   Joel Seidman, "Efforts Toward Merger, 1935-1955." *Industrial and Labor Relations Review* 9 (April 1956): 366.

42.   Goulden, 200. See also AFL-CIO Convention Proceedings, Vol. I, 1967, 391-92 where Meany reiterates this view.

43.   AFL Convention Proceedings, 1955, 5.

44.   Ibid., 406.

45.   Ibid., 356.

46.   John Hutchinson, "The Constitution and Government of the AFL-CIO." *California Law Review* 46 (1958), 740-42; Henry Pelling, *American Labor* (Chicago: University of Chicago Press, 1960), also interprets the merger in this way.

47.   James Q. Wilson, *Political Organizations* (New York: Basic Books, 1974).

48.   "The Merger: Credits and Debits," *The Nation* (December 10, 1955): 505.

49.   *New York Times*, (September 7, 1955).

50.   *New York Times*, (March 3, 1955).

51.   *New York Times*, (December 6, 1955).

52.   *New York Times*, (September 17, 1955).

53.   *New York Times*, (February 11, 1955).

54.   Gall, 110.

3. *A Rope of Sand*

The administrative structure of the new AFL-CIO resembled that of its predecessors. Authority continued to be decentralized, resting in the hands of the affiliated unions rather than the newly merged AFL-CIO.[1] As a result, COPE would lack the authority to command the affiliated unions and would have to persuade them to implement register-and-vote drives, support endorsed candidates, politically educate their members, and collect money on COPE's behalf. Nor could COPE go above the heads of the affiliated unions and organize the membership itself to perform these tasks because COPE lacked the resources to do so. It would have to work through the affiliated and local union leadership over whom it had no formal authority.

Some scholars have dismissed the effect this decentralization of authority and resources within organized labor has had on functional committees like COPE. In his study of a functional committee within the old AFL, Godson found that leaders of the Free Trade Union Committee (FTUC) "were able to accommodate themselves to the relatively light constraints imposed by the organizational environment in which they had to operate."[2] Yet, Godson notes that "Most unions rarely donated more than token amounts per year to FTUC."[3] As a result, FTUC was financially unable to do what was expected of it. And while effective

---

*Portions of this chapter appeared originally in my article "A Rope of Sand: The AFL-CIO Committee on Political Education," *Economic and Industrial Democracy*, Vol. 7, No. 1 (February 1986): 45-61. The author gratefully acknowledges the permission of Sage Publications, Inc. to use this material.

implementation of FTUC's program "required the cooperation of other AFL leaders," Godson found that "affiliated union leaders, as a whole, were uninterested in it."[4] Godson concludes, "Their lack of enthusiasm for international involvement imposed a major constraint on FTUC policy makers."[5] Clearly, the organizational environment that Godson spoke of earlier did have an impact on the FTUC that it could ignore only at its peril. We might well ask whether the organizational environment that COPE encountered had an impact on it similar to the one it had on FTUC? Has COPE's organizational dependence on the affiliated and local union leadership affected its ability to pursue social democratic activities and objectives?

In the conclusion to this chapter it is argued that COPE's decentralized control structure,[6] its dependence on the affiliated unions for cooperation and support, engendered narrow interest group appeals as opposed to the broad class demands suggested by Greenstone. The mutual self-interest of the affiliated unions and the incentives for secondary labor leaders to participate in COPE programs rested far more on appeals that addressed the rights, privileges, and autonomy of trade union organizations than they did on consumer-class demands. Only by appealing to the secondary labor leadership on these narrow institutional grounds could COPE hope to receive their support. The support of secondary labor leaders was, of course, essential because COPE had no way to reach the membership except through them. Thus COPE limited its appeals to those issues it believed would mobilize the secondary leadership on its behalf.

THE POLITICAL ORGANIZATION OF COPE

The national office of COPE is headed by a Director who is appointed by the AFL-CIO president. COPE's national office also originally included a Woman's Activities Department (WAD), a Minorities Department, staff for research and publicity, and area directors who served as the national office's representatives in the field. At the time of the merger, the staff of the national office did not include more than 50 people. With so few staff, the function of the national office was clearly not to perform political work itself, but to coordinate and assist the work of other organizations, especially state and local central bodies.

State and local central bodies attempt to overcome what the Webbs identified as the most serious problem trade unions confront when they try to mobilize politically: trade unions are organized on the basis of trade or industry not voting district.[7] State and local central bodies attempt to address this handicap by coordinating the activity of local unions within a given area. Coordination is required, primarily, for political work as state and local central bodies are barred from involvement in collective bargaining or strikes without the consent of the unions concerned. An AFL-CIO pamphlet describes the role of state and local central bodies in the following manner: "Increased emphasis on political education and legislation has served to point up the vital and essential role of these branches of the AFL-CIO. They are the logical structure in which to build an effective, coordinated COPE program and, in turn, to ensure grass roots support for legislation."[8]

As part of their work, each state and local central body is authorized to organize a COPE committee. These committees are supposed to implement COPE programs of voter education, voter registration, and solicit contributions for COPE. In addition, state central bodies endorse candidates for statewide office and for Congress, while local central bodies endorse candidates for such local offices as mayor or city aldermen. The direction of state and local COPE programs is left to the discretion of state and local central bodies although they must adhere to general rules of conduct prescribed by the AFL-CIO. State and local COPE programs are funded through the treasuries of state and local central bodies, but assistance from national COPE is not unusual.

State Central Bodies

In 1965 AFL-CIO President George Meany told the delegates to the Maryland-D.C. state AFL-CIO convention that, "The state Federations are far more important in political action than the national office in Washington, D.C."[9] He explained that the success of the AFL-CIO's legislative program in Congress depended upon the ability of the state organizations to educate politically and mobilize union members. Yet, state central bodies are a weak link, though not the weakest, within the COPE chain of command. A study by Stephen Cook on the effect of state and local COPE endorsements on the rank and file found, "For the typical union member...State Central Bodies...are likely to be far removed, little understood organizations that are trade union related only in some vague, undefinable fashion."[10] COPE programs run by state central bodies encounter the following problems.

The first problem that limits COPE programs at this level is jurisdictional and representational disputes among affiliated unions and their locals. The merger of AFL and CIO state organizations proceeded much slower than was originally anticipated in the 1955 merger agreement due to the rancor generated by these disputes. At the 1957 AFL-CIO convention, the Building and Construction Trades Department declared, "We sincerely feel that until a mutually agreed upon solution [on jurisdictions] is found there can be no real unity in the labor movement."[11] The merger agreement stated that all AFL and CIO state organizations were to be merged by December, 1957. However, none of the state organizations in the large industrialized states of the Northeast and Midwest, where the union membership was concentrated, were merged by that date. In many states, AFL and CIO state central bodies continued to operate their separate political organizations, LLPE and PAC respectively, rather than join political forces in COPE. Based on his review of the first five years of labor unity, Scott concluded, "the AFL-CIO has still not found a satisfactory method of dealing with these [jurisdictional] issues. Furthermore, merger at the state and local levels, while effective in principle, is ineffective in practice because of overlapping and duplicating efforts that stem from old rivalries."[12]

Jurisdictional and representational disputes have abated but not fully disappeared. They continue to have a baneful effect on political programs run by state labor organizations depriving them of the cooperation and solidarity necessary for success.

A second and far more serious problem that state COPE programs confront is the failure of local unions to affiliate with their state organization. In 1961 a survey of 99 affiliated unions found that only 48.5 percent of their locals were affiliated with their state central body.[13] Despite an intense effort to raise the affiliation rate, rates stabilized at the 50 percent mark in the 1960s and even declined somewhat in the 1970s.[14] Only recently has this decline been reversed.[15] Due to the low affiliation rate of local unions to their state central body these organizations find it difficult to raise the revenue necessary to support a statewide political program. Local unions fail to affiliate with their state central body for various reasons. First, they may view the services provided by the state organization as redundant because they are already contributing to similar programs through their international. Second, local unions may fail to affiliate because they disagree with the policies of the state organization. For instance, in the South during the 1960s, local unions disaffiliated *en masse* from their state organizations to protest the pro-civil rights position taken by their state organizations. Third, some local unions fail to affiliate because they find the per capita tax charged by their state organization burdensome. When the Mississippi state AFL-CIO raised its per capita tax by $1.00 in 1961, the Amalgamated Clothing Workers district director withdrew his locals from the state AFL-CIO because he felt state dues were set too high. Fourth, some local unions fail to support their state organization because they feel it has been captured by unions they view less than favorably.[16] Finally, to add insult to injury, local unions that are affiliated do not always report their full membership to the state organization in order to limit the per capita tax they must pay.

The issue of low affiliation rates to state central bodies is a perennial one that appears frequently at AFL-CIO conventions. But it was raised with particular intensity at the 1959 AFL-CIO convention which occurred following the passage of the Landrum-Griffin Act. At the convention, August Scholle, president of the Michigan state AFL-CIO, offered a resolution that called for the mandatory affiliation of local unions to their state organization. Scholle felt this action would strengthen labor's political organization and prevent such legislative debacles as Landrum-Griffin in the future. He argued:

> Why I hear every International President give the most profound lip service to political action and they make speeches at us time and again saying this is the most important function of the trade union movement....Yet, what do we do? To the very organization which is given the prime responsibility for carrying out these functions we say, 'Well, now. Look, you can pay your dues if you so choose.'[17]

The AFL-CIO's Constitutional Committee recommended that the convention vote against Scholle's proposal. It maintained that mandatory local union affiliation would abridge the power of the affiliated unions and alter the entire structure of the Federation. AFL-CIO President George Meany joined in the debate to defend the recommendation of the Constitutional Committee. A delegate from Maryland responded plaintively to Meany:

> We are attempting to launch a political program. As most of you know we had four defections on the Landrum-Griffin vote....Now we would like to be in a position at least to go back in 1960 with a real fight. We don't have the tools to do so.
> We accept our position as a coordinating group, as a coordinating segment of this great body, but by the same token we have got to have the tools.
> We are dedicated. We want to do a good job. We are dedicated to the labor movement and will continue to be, but we must have some kind of relief....Our most growing weakness [sic] in the state of Maryland is the lack of affiliation in the central level, the city central level and the state level.[18]

A third problem confronted by state COPE programs has been the modernization of state legislatures. In 1960 one-half of all state legislatures met in annual session; a decade later all but ten did. State legislative sessions were not only more frequent but lasted longer. By 1969 presession drafting of bills was permitted in every state but Wyoming, and presession filing of bills was permitted in 26 states.[19] The modernization of state legislatures has forced state labor organizations to divert resources from campaign activity to overseeing the state legislature. Lobbying the state legislature is now a year-round activity that absorbs the political attention and energy of the state central body at the expense of COPE programs.

A final problem that COPE programs confront at the state level is the lack of sanctions available to state central bodies. Affiliated local unions can disregard the directions of the state organization with impunity. A business agent from the International Brotherhood of

Electrical Workers told Kahn:

> My men are first, last and always—electricians. We think
> it pays off to be affiliated with the rest of labor. But if
> there should ever be a serious conflict between us and the
> state organization that couldn't be worked out, then we
> would tell them to go straight to hell. And there isn't a
> damn thing they can do about it....They don't have power
> and they know it.[20]

Without sanctions to compel cooperation and participation in state
COPE programs, these programs are at the mercy of affiliated locals who
contribute money, participate in register-and-vote drives, and distribute
literature at their discretion.   Kahn writes, "The nature of LABOR
permits any union to accept or reject the COPE program as it sees fit; for
as directors of a confederation, the COPE state leadership cannot invoke
sanctions to induce compliance with official policy."[21]

The lack of sanctions available to state AFL-CIOs prevents them
from effectively performing the role for which they were designed: to
coordinate the activities of unions across the various trades. After the
1966 election, one Amalgamated Meatcutters local in Oregon wrote its
international in Chicago, "COPE endorsed Straub and several locals
endorsed McCall....Everyone seemed to want to go their own way.
Apparently they lack confidence in COPE....COPE endorsed Duncan and
the Secretary of one of our locals actively campaigned and made
television appearances for his opponent."[22] The survey of local union
activity in which this account appeared also contained reports from local
unions in New York, Massachusetts, and Indiana who similarly decried
the inability of state organizations to enforce political discipline.   One
union wag at a state council convention used a parable to draw attention
to this problem gently. It seemed the only way to get to heaven was to
ask St. Peter a question he could not answer.   Two well-educated
businessmen whispered a question in St. Peter's ear that he promptly
answered, but when a union man spoke to St. Peter he opened the gate
to heaven and let him in. The two businessmen were very surprised and
asked St. Peter what question the union man had asked that was so
hard that not even St. Peter could answer.   St. Peter replied, "Well, I
don't mind telling you. He asked me when was the labor people going to
get together and I told him I didn't know."[23]

In review, the impediments to an effective state COPE program
are the following: acrimonious jurisdictional disputes that hamper
cooperation between local unions in a common COPE program; the
modernization of state legislatures that strain the already inadequate
resources of state AFL-CIOs; the failure of local unions to affiliate with
their state organization which leaves these organizations underfinanced
and understaffed; the lack of sanctions available to state organizations
which prevents political activity from being coordinated in an effective

manner; and, finally, personal rivalries and plain indifference to political activity on the part of local union leaders.

Local Central Bodies

Local central bodies are more important than the state organizations in political work. They are closer to the membership than the state central bodies and their activities are therefore more visible to the union member. Moreover, state organizations only design and initiate COPE programs, while local central bodies implement them. Local central bodies are supposed to organize door-to-door canvasing and the ward and precinct organization of voters. Kahn writes, "in the specific attempt to register members and get-out-the-vote it is the local COPE which determines success or failure."[24]

Financially, local central bodies are in a less enviable position than the state organizations. At the Idaho state convention in 1974, COPE Area Director Walter Gray commented on the financial condition of local central bodies within the state, "Not one central body can finance their own registration or get-out-the-vote program. Not one is solvent."[25] In response to a proposal by the Kentucky state AFL-CIO that central labor councils begin a registration drive, the president of the Owensboro council replied, "how can the councils expect to do the work you are asking us to do, when in most of the councils throughout the state, their political action money is completely gone."[26] The financial distress of local central bodies is a result of the low per capita fee they levy on affiliated locals and an even lower affiliation rate than that which afflicts state organizations. The failure of local unions to affiliate to their local central body creates the same problems here as it does at the state level. The secretary-treasurer of California Labor COPE stated, "The non-affiliation of some organizations with local COPE...presents almost insurmountable communication problems in developing an effective register-and-vote campaign."[27] At the Maryland State AFL-CIO Convention, the head of the COPE program for one of the regions commented:

> If all of the unions in our area would affiliate with our Council, we could do a much better job. When you have quite a number of local unions who are not affiliated with the Council, and those who are affiliated do not participate in the COPE activities of the Council, it places a double burden on those who are affiliated and are active.[28]

Like state central bodies, local councils lack sanctions over affiliated locals. Local councils thus experience the same problem persuading local unions to respect its endorsements as state organizations have. Asked to identify problems that COPE experienced in his jurisdiction, COPE Area Director Dan Powell wrote the national COPE office, "Even after labor leaders in some cities have made their endorsement, in some instances, labor leaders in some cities and counties still endorse candidates in opposition to the COPE-endorsed candidate."[29] Following the 1966 election, one Amalgamated Meatcutter local was so upset that other local unions did not support the local central body COPE program that it wrote its international it was considering political activity outside of COPE in the future.[30]

While all of the problems which affect state organizations are accentuated at the local council level, this is especially true in the area of staffing. State central bodies either have an officer of the state organization assigned to full-time work directing the COPE program or they hire staff specifically for this purpose. Most local councils do not have full-time officers, let alone staff who can work exclusively on COPE activities. COPE programs at this level thus suffer from a lack of leadership that deprives them of direction and continuity. Moreover, while it is recommended that local councils recruit volunteers to check registration lists and publicize endorsed candidates, these are not forthcoming.

Due to the local council's lack of resources, authority, and leadership, local COPE programs are in a parlous condition. For example, Dan Powell reported that "of the total of 71 CLUs in the 6 states of Area #5, only 48 of these CLUs have a COPE Program....There are 23 which have no COPE Committee, do nothing on COPE, or on anything else....At least one-third of the CLUs in each of my states are either dead or rapidly dying; consequently it is impossible to establish a functioning COPE committee and an effective COPE program in these CLUs."[31]

In California, after a special effort by the state organization to assist its local central bodies, the secretary-treasurer of California Labor COPE Thomas Pitts admitted, "year-round political action programs are still lacking...registration and voter programs are still being conducted on a crash basis....The financing of COPE programs at the local level is far from satisfactory in many areas."[32] Except in cases of unusual perseverance by local council officers, or the concentration of members from one union within a council's jurisdiction, local organizations are overwhelmed by their responsibilities. It is beyond their will and capacity to implement register-and-vote drives, educate the membership, and mobilize them in support of endorsed candidates.

THE ECONOMIC ORGANIZATION OF COPE

Local Union COPE Committees

COPE Committees are supposed to exist within local unions as well as at state and local levels. According to COPE's publication, *How to Win*, "A local union COPE is the heart of any effective political action program."[33] Opportunities for direct and personal contact with the rank and file in order to politically educate and mobilize them are most available here. Yet, despite their proximity to the membership, COPE programs receive little attention within local unions because local union officials lack the will to implement them. One union political representative explained with frustration that for local union officers "politics never has the urgency of everyday bread and butter problems his union faces....Union leaders find the mechanics of shaping a political program dull work. Therefore, it simply doesn't get done."[34] Wolpin found that among the unions he surveyed, the Textile Workers Union, the Amalgamated Clothing Workers Union, and the Retail, Wholesale and Department Store Workers Union, "many locals have yet to create such Committees and many of those which do exist fail to function year-round."[35] In his study of a United Auto Workers local, Norman Blume found that only 15 percent of the 314 members he interviewed could name the candidates their union endorsed.[36] William Form concluded on the basis of his analysis of six studies of local union political activity that "When officials single out "good" or "bad" candidates for public office, members do not know who they are."[37] The following reports of COPE activity at the local union level are typical. The COPE director for the Fifth Congressional District in Kansas lamented:

> ...we seem to have a problem in having local unions answer our correspondence that we send out. We have requested three times, I believe, that the local unions set up their own local union COPEs. We have approximately fifteen local union COPEs set up out of the forty that are affiliated with the State Federation.[38]

His report on attempts to raise money for COPE within local unions was even more discouraging:

> We have found in some of our county meetings that some of our membership—and this might be an awful thing to say but it is true—some of our membership don't even know we have a special drive going on. I know each local union was furnished with these [political contribution receipt] books, was given the information, and somebody stubbed their toe somewhere down the line, apparently the officers of the local unions. We can't expect our members to buy these tickets if they don't know anything about them.[39]

The only way COPE can exert pressure on local unions is through their international. Yet, some internationals are not enthusiastic about promoting COPE. The COPE director for the Second Congressional District in Kansas requested $0.02 per member from locals in his district for political activity. Only 20 percent of the locals responded. In order to increase the response rate he tried to set up a meeting with international representatives and business agents from unions servicing locals in his district. He reported:

> We contacted 43 international representatives and business agents that said they would attend the meeting. Only 3 out of 43 showed up. We have better luck getting the rank and file to our meeting than we do the international representatives and business agents. Our rank and file take more interest in our COPE program than international representatives who should be heading the program and talking and getting people out to vote on election day.[40]

He went on to add that with very little support from the internationals, local unions do not publicize COPE. As a result, little political organizing or education takes place at the level where contact with the membership is most intimate and direct.

The failure of local unions to engage in political education is this level's greatest shortcoming. In his study of the West Virginia state AFL-CIO, Bullard was told by the state COPE director, "the insufficiency of direct communication with the rank and file may be the greatest weakness of COPE."[41] A similar lament was voiced by the Maryland state COPE director, "One of the reasons we have failed...is a lack of communication with the people whom I would love to reach but have no way of reaching."[42] Shop stewards and local union officers are supposed to use their proximity to the membership to conduct political education. Both, however, have been remiss in carrying out their responsibilities.

Shop stewards were regarded by COPE officials at AFL-CIO headquarters as a perfect conduit for political education because their shopfloor duties brought them into personal contact with the rank and file. But the qualities that led COPE to recommend that shop stewards be utilized, their access to members inside the shop in the course of handling workplace grievances, also made them unavailable. It was discovered that performance of their shopfloor responsibilities left them little time for political education.

Local union officers, on the other hand, fail to promote issues or candidates to their members except as they may affect their workplace responsibilities because they lack incentives to do so. They see political work as incidental or only distantly related to their workplace performance to which their own career goals are tied. Furthermore, Bullard found that "because questions of politics are often emotionally charged, local union officers frequently avoid any kind of political question because they fear the loss of their own union office as a result."[43]

CONCLUSION

If AFL-CIO committees like COPE are to fulfill their organizational tasks successfully they must do so in a way which satisfies and placates the affiliated union leadership. COPE is dependent on them for financial and staff support, to inform their members of COPE's endorsements, to get their members to the polls to vote, and to educate them to the policy positions advocated by the AFL-CIO. COPE, however, lacks the authority to compel the participation of the secondary leadership in its activities and it lacks the means to tunnel under them to contact the membership directly. Wolpin writes:

> If the national leadership of the highly autonomous unions which constitute the AFL-CIO have not deemed political action to be sufficiently important to warrant political propagandization efforts within their domains, there is little probability that the aspirations which are trumpeted in Federation and national convention resolutions will occupy any role other than superfluous verbiage.[44]

The same constraints operate at the regional level in the relationship between state and local COPEs and the local union leadership as exist between COPE and the affiliated unions. Both Taft and Kahn observed in their separate studies of the California and Indiana state AFL-CIOs, respectively, that the political activity of the state organization was constrained by its organizational dependence on the affiliated locals.[45] The state AFL-CIO had to move judiciously for fear of antagonizing the support of local union leaders upon whom the success of the state program depended. Kahn writes:

> An organization constructed upon a multiplicity of individual units whose leaders are unchallenged sovereigns within their domains must of necessity take steps with the utmost of caution....Individual leaders who fear any inroads upon their personal prerogatives do not hesitate to withdraw their allegiance from the state organization, and with it financial support.[46]

COPE's response to the organizational constraints it faces have shaped what Fenno calls "the strategic premises" of the organization. By this term, Fenno is referring to ways in which organizations develop modes of behavior which take into account the environmental constraints they face.[47] How has COPE's activity been shaped by its need to satisfy the organizational constraints it faces; its dependence on the cooperation and support of the affiliated and local union leadership? How does COPE seek to manage its environment?

When the AFL and CIO merged, John L. Lewis blessed the new federation by predicting that the merger will part like a rope of sand. Lewis borrowed the colorful phrase "rope of sand" from an earlier remark by Samuel Gompers. Gompers had once defended the decentralized structure of the AFL by claiming that the AFL's lack of centralized authority made it "at once a rope of sand and yet the strongest of human forces—a voluntary association held together by mutual self-interest." According to Gompers, the organizational problems posed by a lack of centralized authority could be overcome easily. The lack of formal administrative channels for the central federation to impose its will upon the affiliates is compensated for by the spontaneous unity that forms out of the affiliated unions pursuing their self-interest. The perceived self-interest of the affiliated unions would induce them to recognize similar needs and coordinate their efforts in lieu of the authoritative direction to do so. Following Gompers's suggestion then, COPE would be able to manage its environment and gain the cooperation and support of the affiliated and local union leadership by appealing to their self-interest. But wherein lies the self-interest of the affiliated unions?

COPE attempts to manage its organizational dependence on the affiliated and local union leadership by appealing to their self-interest in "institutional preservation."[48] The term institutional preservation refers to union support of policies that remove legal restraints on the ability of trade unions to exercise their market power in group conflict with employers and to preserve trade union autonomy. Such issues might include "the right of workers to organize into unions; the right of unions to be recognized by employers as bargaining agents for workers; ...[and] the right of unions to engage in activities necessary to secure equal footing with employers in the workplace...."[49]

Issues other than those that pertain to the institutional preservation or autonomy of trade unions, such as energy policy, protectionism, or other economic policies, create severe obstacles to political unity because of the differential impact such policies have on the market strategies of the affiliated unions. For instance, the United Auto Workers supports import restrictions but such a policy would have dire consequences for the longshoremen. This problem also emerges in the area of energy policy. The building trades unions are proponents of nuclear power because of the enormous construction costs it involves; whereas the Sheet Metal Workers supports solar power because it requires skills utilized by members of this union. This fragments support for such policies within the federation, and since the AFL-CIO is decentralized, it is ill-equipped to overcome such fragmentation. The political unity of unions on issues outside of narrow organizational concerns is thus problematic.

Greenstone, however, argues that welfare state legislation is in the interest of all workers regardless of their trade union affiliation and is thus a demand that could unite the various trades. But the benefits that might be derived from such legislation are often provided to unionized workers through their collective bargaining agreements. As a result, members do not have a stake in such legislation and the local and affiliated union leadership have no incentive to pursue it.

Thus, COPE appeals to the secondary leadership upon whom it is organizationally dependent, on the basis of its self-interest in institutional preservation. Rather than identify the interests of union members in broad class terms, COPE identifies their interests with the autonomy of the trade union organization. Only in this way can it create a political consensus among the secondary leadership and an incentive for them to participate in COPE programs.

As our history of COPE from 1955 to 1967 reveals, COPE was caught tragically between the objectives it was supposed to satisfy and a structure that prevented their realization. On the one hand, COPE was supposed to mobilize the broad constituency of the Democratic party by appealing to their interest in welfare state measures. This would ensure the success of the Democratic party which was essential to preserve the autonomy of trade unions once labor policy had been politicized. On the other hand, the structure of COPE, its dependence on affiliated and local union leaders, precluded support for such social democratic activity and objectives. These leaders, following a market strategy, saw little value in partisan activity except when union autonomy was threatened and saw even less value in encouraging broad support for welfare state measures that were irrelevant to their workplace responsibilities.

NOTES

1. See John Hutchinson, "The Constitution and Government of the AFL-CIO," *California Law Review* 46 (1958), 739-81, for an analysis of the formal organizational structure of the AFL-CIO.

2. Roy Godson, *American Labor and European Politics: The A.F.L. as a Transnational Force* (New York: Crane-Russak, 1976), 46.

3. Ibid., 52.

4. Ibid., 47.

5. Ibid., 47.

6. John D. Stephens, "Class Formation and Class Consciousness: A Theoretical and Empirical Analysis with Reference to Britain and Sweden," *British Journal of Sociology* 30 (December 1979)

also argues that trade union political activity is affected by the degree to which unions are centralized.

7. Beatrice Webb and Sidney Webb, *Industrial Democracy* (London: Longman's, Green & Co., 1926).

8. "The Vital Links," (Washington, D.C.: AFL-CIO, n.d.).

9. Maryland State and D.C. AFL-CIO Convention Proceedings, 1965, 36.

10. Stephen L. Cook, *What is the Impact of State and Local Central Body Endorsement on the Rank and File?* (Morgantown, West Virginia: Institute for Labor Studies, 1975), 9.

11. AFL-CIO Convention Proceedings, Vol. II, 1957, 341.

12. Ebbin Pina Scott, "The AFL-CIO Merger: Unity Accomplishments," (Masters thesis, University of Maryland, 1961), 42.

13. Stanton Smith to National and International Unions and State and Local Central Bodies, February 8, 1961, in AFL-CIO Library, Washington, D.C., Drawer: "S-Central Bodies-State and Local, Folder: "AFL-CIO State and Local Central Bodies.

14. *AFL-CIO News*, (December 10, 1977).

15. *AFL-CIO News*, (November 23, 1981).

16. Frank Hester, "Ohio Labor and Political Action," *Political Affairs* 41 (November 1962): 13-25.

17. AFL-CIO Convention Proceedings 1959, Vol. I, 353.

18. Ibid., 364.

19. Kenneth Palmer, *State Politics in the United States* (New York: St. Martin's Press, 1970), 70.

20. Melvin Kahn, *The Politics of American Labor: The Indiana Microcosm* (Carbondale: Southern Illinois University Labor Institute, 1970), 10.

21. Ibid., 92.

22. "COPE: Amalgamated Meat Cutters and Butcher Workmen of North America," in Dan Powell Papers, Folder 205, Southern Historical Collection, Library of the University of North Carolina, Chapel Hill, N.C.

23. Alabama Labor Council Special Convention Proceedings, 1958, 30.

24. Kahn, 94.

25. Idaho State AFL-CIO Convention Proceedings, 1974, 93.

26. Kentucky State AFL-CIO Convention Proceedings, 1970, 42.

27. California Labor COPE Pre-Primary Convention Proceedings, 1962, 155.

28. Maryland State and D.C. AFL-CIO Convention Proceedings, 1969, 63.

29. Dan Powell to Al Barkan (November 23, 1962) in Dan Powell Papers, Folder 197.

30. "COPE: Amalgamated Meat Cutters and Butcher Workmen of North America," *op. cit.*

31. "Summary of State Reports for 1968," Daniel A. Powell to Joseph M. Rourke (January 30, 1969) in Dan Powell Papers, Folder 6.

32. California Labor COPE, Pre-Primary Convention Proceedings and Reports, 1962, 55.

33. "How to Win," (Washington, D.C.: AFL-CIO, 1964), 19.

34. Dick Bruner, "Labor Should Get Out of Politics" *Harper's Magazine* 217 (April 1958): 25.

35. Miles Wolpin, "Factors Influencing Labor's Internal Political Cohesion," (Masters thesis, Columbia University, 1964), 25.

36. Norman Blume, "The Impact of a Local Union on its Membership in a Local Election" *Western Political Quarterly* 22 (1970): 143.

37. William Form, *Divided We Stand: Working Class Stratification in America* (Urbana, Ill.: University of Illinois Press, 1985), 202.

38. Kansas Federation of Labor Convention Proceedings, 1960, 64.

39. Ibid., 64.

40. Ibid., 68.

41. Todd Bullard, *Labor and the Legislature* (Morgantown, West Virginia: Bureau for Government Research, 1965), 102.

42. Maryland State and D.C. AFL-CIO Convention Proceedings, 1969, 48.

43. Bullard, 102.

44. Wolpin, 139.

45. Philip Taft, *Labor Politics American Style: The California State Federation of Labor* (Cambridge: Harvard University Press, 1968); Kahn, *op. cit.*

46. Kahn, 75.

47. Richard Fenno, *Congressmen in Committees* (Boston: Little, Brown & Co., 1973), xv; 46-47.

48. V. L. Allen, "The Centennial of the British T.U.C.: 1868-1968" in John Saville and Ralph Miliband, eds., *Socialist Register, 1968* (New York: Monthly Review Press, 1968), 231-52.

49. Gwendolyn Mink, *Old Labor and New Immigrants in American Political Development* (Ithaca: Cornell University Press, 1986), 40.

4. *The Formative Years*

In its first five years of operation, COPE's attention was divided equally between mobilizing the AFL-CIO membership in elections and overcoming the organizational obstacles placed in COPE's path by the decentralized structure of the AFL-CIO. Two events contributed to the solution of both of these challenges. The first was the threat to union security posed by the campaign rhetoric of the Republican party in 1958 and the number of right-to-work proposals considered in states that same year. Affiliated and local union leaders sought refuge in COPE from these threats to union security. They complied with COPE requests to educate their members to the issues at stake in the election and to coordinate their activity through state and local central bodies.

The second event was the passage of the Labor-Management Reporting and Disclosures Act (LMRDA), popularly known as the Landrum-Griffin Act, which further politicized the field of labor relations. The internal governance of trade unions was now a matter of public policy. In response to the Act's passage, COPE received financial and staff assistance from unions that had not contributed previously. COPE was supported initially by unions from the old CIO and only a handful of former AFL unions. Now, as a result of Landrum-Griffin, COPE received support from all sections of the AFL-CIO.

Furthermore, as a result of the passage of the Landrum-Griffin Act, COPE made preparations to mobilize not only union members but the wider Democratic party constituency for the 1960 elections. COPE aggregated voters, especially blacks, into the Democratic party, not out of a concern with lofty welfare state objectives, but because the handling of union finances, the legality of union constitutions, and the election of trade union officials were all now subject to political regulation. The pursuit of union security and institutional autonomy, would be sought through social democratic means: aggregating voters outside the AFL-

CIO membership into the Democratic party.

This chapter will be divided into two sections. The first section will describe COPE's activity between 1956 and 1959. The second section will examine COPE's voter aggregation activity in the 1960 elections.

THE FORMATIVE YEARS

On February 14, 1956, the merger of the AFL's LLPE and the CIO's PAC took place without incident. It was decided in the merger discussions that the staffs of both organizations would be retained. But, representatives from the AFL and CIO disagreed intensely over who would direct the new committee. CIO unions lobbied for Jack Kroll, former director of PAC, to be named director of COPE. They were proud of the national reputation PAC enjoyed as an electoral force. They also felt that if an AFL man was given this position COPE would not be as vital or as active as PAC had been. AFL unions, on the other hand, recommended Jim McDevitt, director of LLPE, to fill this sensitive post. They favored the low-key approach of LLPE in comparison to the public campaigns of PAC and were skeptical of PAC's close identification with the Democratic party. Both sides were uncompromising. To resolve the dispute, the new AFL-CIO President George Meany appointed Kroll and McDevitt as co-directors of COPE. This solution distinguished COPE as the only department in the new AFL-CIO that would have its leadership split down the middle between former CIO and AFL division heads. By compromising between AFL and CIO recommendations in this manner, Meany hoped to secure the loyalty of both AFL and CIO unions to the new organization. CIO unions would feel confident that their point of view was represented within COPE by Kroll, just as AFL unions would feel secure that McDevitt was overseeing political operations. Richard McSorley from the Lathers Union of the old AFL and Al Barkan from the Textile Workers Union of the CIO were named assistant directors. This pattern of distributing leadership positions within COPE between the AFL and CIO sides of the federation was continued in later years. When Kroll retired in 1957, Barkan was placed second in command to McDevitt and given the title of deputy director of COPE. Barkan's appointment insured CIO unions of continuing representation at COPE's top levels. When McDevitt died in 1963, Barkan succeeded him as director and Joe Rourke from the IBEW was appointed assistant director. Patronage between building trades and former CIO unions was distributed in this manner so as to tie the more powerful affiliates of the AFL-CIO to COPE. With their representatives holding leadership positions, fears these unions might have that their views were unrepresented would be assuaged. They would thus feel more comfortable in participating in COPE register-and-vote drives and in contributing money. This, of course, is essential because COPE lacks authority to coerce their cooperation.[1]

Financial problems also arose at the start due to the different methods COPE's predecessors had used to raise money. CIO members were conditioned to contribute to PAC through their unions whereas AFL unions had no tradition for soliciting money from their members for political work.[2] As a result, the financial burden for COPE was, initially, carried by unions from the old CIO. In 1956 former CIO unions raised twice as much money for COPE than AFL unions although CIO unions had only half as many members. This brought a chorus of complaints to Meany from CIO unions that felt they were bearing an unfair share of COPE's expenses. Meany replied that AFL unions needed time to accustom their members to contribute to COPE. AFL unions had to first build the network for soliciting contributions within their local unions that CIO locals already had in place. As a gesture to CIO unions, however, Meany declared that after the 1956 election COPE's operating expenses would come out of the AFL-CIO treasury instead of from contributions COPE received from the affiliated unions. Thus, AFL unions would be forced to finance COPE through their AFL-CIO dues. Meany hoped this would placate CIO unions until unions from the old AFL could set up appropriate procedures within their locals to solicit money for COPE.[3]

In 1956 staff from the COPE national office traveled across the country to acquaint trade unionists with the new organization and to prepare for the 1956 elections. COPE staff appeared at the merger conventions of AFL and CIO state and local organizations, at union conventions, and at separate CIO and AFL functions. Conferences in Pittsburgh, New Haven, Chicago, Des Moines, Portland, and San Francisco were held to educate local leaders to the tasks ahead in the upcoming elections. Wherever COPE staff appeared, they urged AFL and CIO local union leaders to cooperate with each other in the approaching election. Political cooperation in the election ahead, they argued, should be the first step toward official merger of AFL and CIO local unions at state and local levels.

Of the many speeches that Kroll and McDevitt delivered in 1956, two are particularly instructive. Kroll spoke to an audience at Oberlin College while McDevitt addressed the Pulp, Sulphur, and Paper Workers convention. In each case the COPE co-directors tried to disabuse their audience of the erroneous notion of COPE that each held. Students and faculty at Oberlin did not distinguish between trade union political activity and partisan activity while union delegates at the Paper Workers convention suffered from the opposite illusion and saw no relationship between them.

At Oberlin, Kroll spoke to the perennial question of whether COPE would develop beyond its trade union base to become the spearhead of a third party movement. To envision such possibilities, argued Kroll, was to confuse the tail of the labor movement for its head. He described COPE's goal as one that supported and complimented the collective bargaining activities of the affiliated unions. He told his audience:

> I think it should be made quite clear that the political arm of the labor movement is an arm only. Our objective is not basically a political objective. It is a trade union objective. We exist to serve the trade union movement, to protect it from attack in the legislative halls of the country, to achieve those of its goals that cannot be achieved through collective bargaining....Our function and our sole aim is to serve the trade union movement....Our success or failure is measured in terms of the trade union movement. It is not measured by the election or defeat of any particular party or...of any particular candidate.[4]

While Kroll was trying to convince a college audience that COPE existed to serve the collective bargaining goals of the affiliated unions and not broader ideological objectives, McDevitt faced a different problem before the Paper Workers. Here, he tried to combat "the unfortunate, regrettable impression" trade unionists had that political activity was separate from responsible trade unionism. McDevitt explained that political activity was essential because "They [public officials] have the power to enact laws that curb or restrict what we believe are our Constitutional rights in the field of collective bargaining." Thus, argued McDevitt, COPE deserved the union's support and cooperation.[5]

In February 1956, COPE made its first presentation before the Executive Council of the AFL-CIO. Council members Maurice Hutcheson of the Carpenters Union and Dave Beck of the Teamsters, both Republicans, did not attend. At the meeting, Kroll analyzed labor's prospects in the upcoming elections. Kroll felt that the greatest danger the labor movement faced in 1956 was "overconfidence". State and local mergers would unite labor while farmers were prepared to bolt the Republican party due to their dissatisfaction with the decline in food prices. In addition, Kroll reasoned that labor's political fortunes would improve just based on the laws of chance alone. With over 65 percent of the marginal seats in Congress held by Republicans, Democrats stood to gain if they could simply break even in these competitive districts. Looking at the distribution of marginal seats between the two parties, that is, those seats in which the candidate last won with less than a five percent plurality, COPE found 11 Republican Senators and only five Democrats held such seats. Those Republican Senators that COPE felt were particularly vulnerable included Wallace Bennett (Utah), James Duff (Pennyslvania), Thomas Kuchel (California), Prescott Bush (Connecticut), Everett Dirkson (Illinois), Bourke Hickenlooper (Iowa), John Butler (Maryland), Homer Capehart (Indiana), Frank Carlson (Kansas), and Eugene Milliken (Colorado). In the House, the story was much the same. There were 93 marginal seats and Republicans held 60 of them. If the Democrats could split in these marginal districts Kroll felt that organized labor would be rewarded with a friendly Congress. Kroll even went so far as to speculate that President Eisenhower would choose not to run for reelection due to reasons of health.[6]

An article by Kroll and McDevitt in the *American Federationist* kicked off COPE's campaign drive for 1956. They argued that members should contribute to COPE because the more unions were free from punitive legislation to pursue collective bargaining, the more members would benefit personally by receiving higher wages. By contributing to COPE, the membership could secure the integrity of their union organization, thereby permitting it to win benefits for them in collective bargaining. Kroll and McDevitt wrote:

> You vote on issues that affect your pocketbook when you cast your ballot at the precinct polling place. If you elect enough of labor's friends, laws that hinder your union in its efforts to win you a pay increase—such as the Taft-Hartley Act and the so-called right-to-work law will be repealed....
>
> Labor increasingly is recognizing that economic and political problems are inseparable. Gains won on the picket line can be taken away by Congress, a state legislature or a local council.[7]

Each union was given a quota it was supposed to raise for COPE based on $1.00 from 25 percent of its membership. In this manner, COPE hoped to have $3,000,000 available for the 1956 election.

The campaign that COPE waged in 1956 was a desultory one, and the results were equally disappointing. Kroll's report to the Executive Committee in February was unduly optimistic. The Eighty-fifth Congress was rated no more favorable to labor by COPE than the Congress it had just replaced. President Eisenhower handily defeated AFL-CIO-endorsed Adlai Stevenson for a second term. As for the campaign, the same duplication of effort and internecine strife which had characterized organized labor's political work prior to the merger were still very much in evidence. Republican members of the AFL-CIO Executive Council, Hutcheson and Beck, were joined by Richard Gray, president of the AFL-CIO Building and Construction Trades Department, and Harry Lundberg of the Seafarer's Union in campaigning publicly for Eisenhower despite the AFL-CIO's endorsement of Stevenson. The Teamsters and Carpenters kept their local unions out of COPE registration and fund-raising drives entirely.[8]

COPE's efforts were stymied by the slow pace at which the merger of AFL and CIO state and local central bodies was proceeding. Jurisdictional conflicts, disputes over the distribution of patronage in the merged state organizations, and personal rivalries all acted to delay state and local mergers. Only in a few states did local unions follow the advice of Kroll and McDevitt and cooperate in campaign work as a prelude to official merger. In Louisiana, AFL and CIO local unions joined forces politically in order to overturn a recently passed right-to-work law. Louisiana AFL and CIO state councils merged soon thereafter. Cooperation also occurred in other Western and Southern states where labor had always been weak. But throughout the Northeast and Midwest, where the union membership was concentrated, AFL and CIO organizations waged separate campaigns. In Illinois the CIO supported the Democratic gubernatorial candidate, Richard B. Austin, while the AFL endorsed his opponent, William Stratton. AFL and CIO endorsements also clashed in the Ohio and Michigan gubernatorial races.[9] The New York State CIO council invited AFL unions to participate in joint campaign work but only IBEW locals responded to their offer. In Pittsburgh the CIO central labor council endorsed Democrats in every race but one, while the AFL central council endorsed seven GOP candidates.[10] In Indiana, one of the Republican Senators whom Kroll had earlier designated as vulnerable, Homer Capehart, circulated a letter of endorsement furnished him by Richard Gray, president of the AFL-CIO Building and Construction Trades Department. Kroll and McDevitt tried to put their finger in the dike and wrote a letter "To all former AFL Local Union," urging them "to ignore Mr. Gray's letter. It, we are sure, does not represent the thinking of the General Presidents of the 19 Building Trade Unions nor of the overwhelming majority of the members of the Building and Construction Trades."[11] Trouble with the building trades also occurred in California. Kroll had earlier designated Thomas Kuchel as one of the vulnerable Republican Senators who COPE wanted to see replaced. Kuchel, however, received the support of the building trades because he favored applying Davis-Bacon prevailing wage requirements to proposed federal highway construction.

COPE could not contain these types of forces. Subscribing to a market strategy, each union calculated its political interests based upon the particular needs of its trade. Without issues in the campaign that could spontaneously unite and mobilize the affiliated unions, they responded politically according to their own economic interest, if they responded at all. Kroll and McDevitt tried to put the best face on the 1956 results and described them as the "equivalent of a win." They argued that "In no instance did any major candidate for a major office campaign successfully on an anti-union program. All successful candidates at least paid lip service to trade unionism and to the principles of trade unionism." Second, a Democratic Congress was returned to office despite Eisenhower's landslide victory. Meany considered this "little short of a political miracle."[12] Finally, COPE was encouraged by signs that merger did pay off politically. COPE fared best in states west of the Mississippi where the greatest progress toward state and local mergers had taken place. COPE's Preliminary Analysis of the election found that "in those states in which labor unity has been achieved, the greatest political successes were achieved. In those states where there is still antagonism between former AFL and former CIO groups there was less success."[13] This was a hopeful sign for the future. The Preliminary Analysis also noted that where sharp labor issues were posed, as in Louisiana, Colorado, Washington, and Oregon, state and local COPEs mobilized effectively and successfully.[14]

In conclusion, the 1956 election was noteworthy for the lack of cooperation COPE received from the affiliated unions in its first electoral effort. The merger of LLPE and PAC into COPE did nothing to condense the political interests of the affiliated unions. As a result, COPE could not contain the centrifugal forces created by each union acting in the political arena to further its own economic objectives. Conflicting endorsements and unions that conducted political operations outside of COPE were the result. The merger of LLPE and PAC into COPE simply brought the different political interests of the affiliated unions under one roof, but did nothing to resolve or synthesize them. Organizationally dependent on the affiliates, COPE's performance in 1956 reflected the disunity that results when each union pursues its market needs in the political arena.

In 1957 COPE tried to repair the organizational cracks that appeared in the 1956 campaign. At the second Industrial Unions Department (IUD) convention, COPE Assistant Director Al Barkan told the delegates that COPE was in trouble "because of our own political and organizational shortcomings."[15] According to Barkan, local unions did not distribute COPE literature, check the registration status of their members, or solicit contributions for COPE as was requested of them. In 1956 COPE only attained 47.7 percent of the quota it had set for the unions, $200,000 less than LLPE and PAC raised separately in 1952. Only a handful of AFL unions responded to COPE's appeal for funds; of the $823,718 it collected in the campaign, only $538,598 came in the form of voluntary contributions from the membership.[16] The rest of the money that COPE received took the form of donations from union treasuries. Part of the reason why local union collections among the membership were inadequate was that the affiliated unions failed to provide sufficient leadership to members on this matter. The problem, said Barkan, was not that members did not want to contribute to COPE, but that they were not asked. The affiliates needed to apply more pressure on their local unions to see that they complied with COPE's program.[17] A survey of forty-five affiliated unions supported Barkan's complaint. The survey found that some local unions had developed excellent COPE programs, some had none at all, and some locals only made an effort as election day approached.[18]

In January 1957, the Executive Council met to consider the same problem that Barkan raised at the IUD convention: the lack of money netted in COPE's dollar drive. It issued a statement urging all affiliates who did not fully meet their 1956 quota to submit the balance to COPE at this time. Other technical problems were also addressed. The 1956 campaign revealed that registration activity was often conducted on a "crash basis" as registration deadlines approached. The Executive Council maintained that registration programs had to be conducted year-round if they were to be effective.[19] In March, Meany sent a letter to all affiliated unions requesting that they monitor whether local unions complied with the council's request. At the same time, Kroll and McDevitt wrote to all central labor bodies urging them to establish registration committees in their districts. COPE area conferences in the spring carried these messages to labor leaders across the country.

The 1956 campaign indicated that forces from outside the labor movement were needed to stimulate the secondary leadership to support and coordinate their activity through COPE. COPE lacked the authority and resources to generate this enthusiasm itself. Fortuitously, events in 1958 supplied COPE with the spark it needed: a plethora of right-to-work amendments appeared on various state ballots; Republican party campaign rhetoric threatened trade union autonomy; and, finally, union leaders viewed continuing congressional investigations into union corruption as cynical attempts to lay the groundwork for more restrictive labor legislation. Affiliated and local union leaders sought shelter in COPE from these assaults upon the labor movement as a whole.

COPE entered 1958 optimistic about its electoral prospects. McDevitt, now sole director of COPE following Kroll's retirement in 1957, cited three reasons why COPE would have more success in 1958 than it had in its first electoral campaign.[20] First, merger at the state and local levels was almost complete. By November 1958, only four AFL and CIO state organizations had not yet merged. Furthermore, some state organizations had even gone ahead and hired staff to develop statewide COPE programs as Kroll and McDevitt had requested. The foundation for the coordination of AFL and CIO political activity at state and local levels was now in place.

Another reason for optimism, argued McDevitt, was that the economy was in its worst recession since the Depression. Between the third quarter of 1957 and the first quarter of 1958, Gross National Product fell $20 billion. Industrial production and business expenditures for new plants and equipment declined markedly, as did corporate profits. Seasonally adjusted unemployment averaged 7.2 percent between March and August 1958. McDevitt felt this downturn in business activity would place great strain on the union leadership in collective bargaining. Union leaders would be under pressure to win contracts that could keep pace with inflation while unemployment continued to rise. McDevitt forecast that President Eisenhower's failure to resort to counter-cyclical economic policies would increase the interest of the affiliated union leadership in the forthcoming elections and in COPE.

Lastly, McDevitt felt that Republican attempts to make the alleged power of unions a major campaign theme in 1958 would also stimulate union political activity. Republican party rhetoric during the 1958 campaign was unrelenting in its attack upon unions. *Business*

Week reported, "Whatever the reason for it, labor's emergence as one of the top issues in the 1958 campaign has put unions further on the defensive than they have been since 1947. The national appeals to voters to curb labor have been so strong and so widespread—and the unions feel so subtly pervasive—that the unions are campaigning more to hold their present position than to extend their lines further."[21]

The attempt to curb unions was not reserved for rhetoric alone. In 1957, 13 state legislatures considered outlawing the union shop. But more frightening than this development was the location of states where right-to-work laws were debated seriously. No longer was right-to-work confined to Southern and Plains states where labor was known to be weak. Now it spread into the large industrial states of the Northeast and Midwest as well. Indiana passed a right-to-work measure in 1957. In Connecticut, a right-to-work bill reached the stage of a vote in the state legislature. Bills to outlaw the closed shop were also filed in Delaware, Rhode Island, and Maryland. Moreover, in 1958, right-to-work amendments were scheduled to appear as referendum proposals on the ballot in six states: California, Kansas, Ohio, Washington, Colorado, and Idaho.

McDevitt accurately forecast the union response to these threats. In 1956 COPE showed strength in the West. In 1958 COPE made gains in the Midwest and Northeast as the threat to union security was nationalized by Republican campaign rhetoric and the extension of right-to-work proposals into the industrial heartland. More labor-endorsed candidates were successful in 1958 than in any year since 1948. COPE-endorsed candidates were victorious in 17 out of 33 gubernatorial races and in 60 percent of the House races where endorsements were issued. Twenty-three out of thirty COPE endorsed Senate candidates won seats in the Eighty-seventh Congress. The Senate "Class of '58" included such liberal Democrats as Gale McGee (Wyoming), Philip Hart (Michigan), Stephen Young (Ohio), Vance Hartke (Idaho), Edmund Muskie (Maine), Eugene McCarthy, (Minnesota), and Frank Moss (Utah). Right-to-work amendments lost in five of the six states where they appeared on the ballot. After the election the *Wall Street Journal* editorialized that "COPE, the political arm of the AFL-CIO, was the true winner at the polls in November."[22]

Many factors contributed to the success of COPE-endorsed liberal Democrats in the election: traditional midterm losses for the Presidential party, the 1957-58 recession, and the dissaffection of farmers with the Republican party due to a drop in farm prices. But the energetic, resourceful activity of local unions and state and local COPE committees also contributed to the overwhelming Democratic victory. Political interest within unions was at a peak. Twenty COPE area conferences were held in 1958 with attendance increasing threefold over the previous year. Conference discussions and presentations concentrated on how unions could defend themselves politically from right-to-work proposals. Area conferences also reviewed the problems COPE had encountered in

1956:   a lack of local central body organization, business agents who were indifferent to COPE requests, the lack of money netted in COPE's dollar drive, and local union leaders who were afraid to educate their member politically because their stand might be "unpopular with their members and they won't be elected when they run again."[23]

The degree to which threats to union security stimulated COPE activity can best be seen in the states where right-to-work amendments appeared on the ballot or had been enacted recently.   Cumulatively, in these states (California, Ohio, Washington, Colorado, Idaho, Kansas, and Indiana) all 4 COPE endorsed Senate candidates won, 5 out of 6 COPE-endorsed gubernatorial candidates were victorious and Democrats gained control of each state house, except in Kansas where Democrats took 14 seats from the Republicans.

In California both Republican gubernatorial and senate candidates, William F. Knowland and Goodwin Knight, respectively, credited their defeats to the work of trade unions within their state. Knight recalled that the unions "regarded this as a struggle for their very existence [and] were determined that not only would labor register everybody, but they would vote everybody."[24]   Not only were trade unions agitated by the right-to-work amendment, but Knowland made the alleged power of trade unions the dominant theme of his campaign. In response, organized labor made "the greatest effort in its history in this campaign."[25]   They "exhibited far greater organization, keener management in strategic and tactical planning and more lavish financing than in any previous election."[26]   Unlike 1956, AFL and CIO local unions in California worked together in 1958 in the battle against the right-to-work amendment.   Financially, local unions raised over $2,000,000 to defeat the right-to-work referendum proposal. Registration statewide increased 300,000 over 1956, with 70 percent of the new registrants filing as Democrats due, in part, to trade union efforts. This made possible the record number of votes in California cast on election day.

The degree to which threats to union security were responsible for the unions' vigorous activity in the 1958 election can be seen in the decay of COPE programs once the right-to-work amendment was defeated. The California state AFL-CIO was unable to sustain the level of political organization and activity it reached in 1958. In 1962 Secretary-Treasurer of California Labor COPE Thomas Pitts reported, "After the general elections [of 1958] there was a general deterioration of COPE effort."[27] The number of active local central body COPE committees in California declined from 19 in 1958 to 7 in 1961. At the California Labor COPE Pre-Primary Convention in 1962, Roy Reuther admonished the delegates:

...in order to get the job done must the labor movement
have to have a right-to-work fight in which it gets its back
to the wall....

I was out here in 1958 and I know business agents that were interested and active that haven't done a thing on voter registration this year.

I have not seen a sense of urgency in this campaign. I have not seen a total mobilization on registration.[28]

In Ohio where a right-to-work amendment also appeared on the state ballot, the pace of COPE activity matched that of California. In the gubernatorial race, Republican incumbent Richard O'Neill identified himself with the open shop amendment and lost to Michael DiSalle. Two years earlier O'Neill had defeated DiSalle by 427,000 votes. DiSalle carried every county that voted "no" on the right-to-work amendment while O'Neill won 16 of the 19 counties that voted "yes." Election returns in the senate race also followed the right-to-work vote closely. Stephen Young upset Republican incumbent John Bricker who had not lost a statewide election in 22 years. Bricker carried all 19 counties that voted for the right-to-work amendment, but only 3 of the 16 that voted against it. Young's plurality in such traditional Democratic party strongholds as Cuyahoga (Cleveland), Lucas (Toledo), and Mahoning (Youngstown) counties was over 175,000 votes, with large turnouts reported from each county. Later, Young attributed his victory to the "large turnout of voters brought out by the failure of the Republicans and the right-to-work proposal."[29] The Democrats also took 36 seats in the Ohio state house, changing a Republican majority of 55 seats to a 19 seat advantage for the Democrats. The Ohio state senate also changed hands from a 22-12 seat advantage for the Republicans to a 21-13-seat majority for the Democrats. Finally, in the right-to-work referendum, Ohio voters rejected the right-to-work proposal by the largest margin ever recorded an issue on the ballot in the state's history.

Here, as occurred in California, the right-to-work issue stimulated union activity and contributed to the statewide Democratic sweep. First, the open shop measure temporarily distracted AFL and CIO local unions in Ohio from their acrimonious quarreling. In February 1958, they met to form United Organized Labor of Ohio (UOLO) to combat the right-to-work proposal. At the meeting, state AFL and CIO representatives drafted strategy and made preparations to conduct joint registration drives and publicity. According to Miller and Ware, "policy making in UOLO appeared untouched by dissension."[30] Three months after this initial meeting to form UOLO, AFL and CIO state organizations in Ohio officially merged.

Miller and Ware report "Organized labor probably did the best job it ever did in registering families and their members."[31] Volunteers checked registration rolls to spot unregistered union members and they canvassed neighborhoods. Due to their efforts, a record number of registrants for an off-year election filed with the Board of Elections. The Democratic Party reaped the benefit of this effort, because—as occurred in California—a majority of these new registrants filed as Democrats.

The right-to-work issue also saw Ohio unions extend efforts beyond their own membership to include groups within the Democratic party coalition.   Phil Weightman, COPE Field Director in charge of minority programs, was brought in from the national COPE office in Washington, D.C. to work the black precincts.   Barber shops, beauty parlors, social clubs, churches, ministers and civic leaders in black communities were enlisted to take part in "Operation Registration." "Freedom buses" were organized by the NAACP, COPE, and local ministers to take new registrants to the Board of Elections.   Bus schedules were announced from church pulpits.   COPE also paid canvassers to go door-to-door in black neighborhoods to check if occupants were registered.   COPE literature addressed to the black community argued that the same people who supported right-to-work in Ohio were responsible for the defeat of Fair Employment Practices legislation in the Ohio state legislature. Weightman wrote McDevitt that more than 40,000 blacks were newly registered as a result of these efforts.[32] COPE was repaid for its efforts. Black districts voted eight-to-one against right-to-work.[33]

As was the case in California, once the right-to-work amendment was defeated "much of the organization...of the 1958 campaign... disappeared rapidly after the election."[34]   Overtures to potential allies outside the labor movement came to a halt.   Weightman's hopes that Ohio labor would "participate in every phase of community life to let people know that we are aware of their problems and that we are concerned and grateful for the confidence shown" were not realized. From retirement in Cincinnati, Kroll wrote McDevitt:

> In 1958, in the "right-to-work" campaign in Ohio, we set up a State Central Office and a large State Committee who met frequently to devise plans and propaganda, and enlisted thousands of officers and members alike to spread the propaganda, to all corners of the State. Finances were raised by the State and distributed wherever the Central Committee decided it was needed. In the 1960 campaign there were just two State Central Committee meetings held and both were short meetings. One was for the endorsement of candidates, and the other a general meeting sparsely attended, to get out the vote. There was none or little attempt to raise money and that which was received from the outside, was distributed through local pressures, or for other reasons, resulted in each community's International or Local Unions doing an effective job or very little just as they determined.[35]

In the Senate race in Indiana, Vance Hartke defeated Governor Harold Handley by the largest margin in Indiana senatorial history. In

1957, Handley had made himself the target of the newly merged Indiana state AFL-CIO when he permitted a right-to-work bill passed by the state legislature to become law without his signature. Reporting from Indiana to the national COPE office, COPE area director Dan Powell wrote that "Labor's total political effort in terms of time, effort, manpower and money has by far exceeded that of any previous election."[36] Powell went on to report that merger and post-merger problems, which previously hampered COPE in Indiana, had been overcome by a new spirit of cooperation and unity among local unions in the state. As was true in neighboring Ohio, right-to-work directed union energies at Republicans instead of at each other. Moreover, local union political activity was at a peak. Indiana labor spent $85,000 in the campaign and 1,800 COPE volunteers were expected to help get the vote out on election day. In Indianapolis, the Steelworkers carried out their first search of the registration rolls to identify unregistered members, local unions in Fort Wayne conducted their first registration campaign, and support for Republicans among building trades unions in the state showed a noticeable decline.[37]

Given the nature of the threats the labor movement faced in 1958, its political activism is unsurprising. What needs to be more fully explained is the partisan shape this mobilization took. The Democratic party was the beneficiary of COPE's increased efforts. This was especially true in states where Democratic party candidates rode the coattails of trade union mobilization on the right-to-work issue. The assistance that COPE gave the party as a result of political threats to union security was of three kinds.

First, the impetus to labor unity caused by the assault on trade union rights unified Democratic party organizations in many states. Previously, divisions within organized labor had been, in part, responsible for the weak and incoherent statewide organization of the Democratic party in Indiana and Ohio. But with the right-to-work issue unifying the unions, Democratic party organization also became more cohesive.

Second, the unions expanded their political activities beyond the trade union membership to include groups within the Democratic party coalition. COPE conducted register-and-vote drives among minorities in states where union security was threatened. Through such drives among minorities the unions hoped to expand the base of the Democratic party. Goodwin Knight, the defeated Republican senatorial candidate from California said, "they [unions] not only gave tremendous support to the Democratic candidates, but they registered literally hundreds of thousands of people who never voted before."[38]

Third, right-to-work spurred the unions to solidify their own internal organization. This was especially true at the critical local union level. The local union leadership diligently executed COPE programs and responded to COPE appeals for assistance because they saw their own prerogatives threatened by restrictive legislation. Passage of a right-to-work amendn ent might mean the loss of members and weaken workplace solidarity. As a result of these pressures, local union leaders assigned staff to check the registration status of their members, they solicited contributions from their members for COPE, and they opened their treasuries to subsidize COPE expenses.

In conclusion, the 1958 election reveals how sensitive COPE is to threats to union security. These threats appeared not only in the guise of right-to-work referenda, but Republican party campaign rhetoric, and fears concerning the actual intent of congressional investigations into union corruption. The affiliates sought refuge in COPE from these threats to the labor movement as a whole. Local union leaders mobilized their members—as well as other social groups—and coordinated their activity through COPE. The Democratic party reaped the harvest of COPE's work, especially where right-to-work referendums appeared on the ballot.

The 1958 election results emboldened the political spirits of the labor leadership. The AFL-CIO Executive Council announced that "constructive labor reform legislation and major revision of the Taft-Hartley Act" were to be given "high priority on labor's legislative agenda for 1959."[39] Meany boasted in the pages of the *Commercial and Financial Chronicle* that "The recent campaign indicates that we are becoming more proficient in the field of politics." He blamed the defeat of Republican candidates in 1958 on their identification with right-to-work proposals and the smear campaign they conducted against unions. He then cautioned that if the attacks against union security continued labor might be forced to "start a political party and do a good job of it."[40] McDevitt was also pleased with the results and how COPE had performed in the election. Organizationally, he noted, COPE had made great progress since 1956. Registration activity was well organized; alliances to the general community had been forged; contributions to COPE had increased during a midterm election, open shop amendments had been defeated in five out of six states; and political success in states that merged continued to demonstrate the value of merger.[41] However, within nine months Meany called the election results, "one of the greatest disillusionments in modern history," and COPE was to be scrutinized closely at the AFL-CIO convention in September.[42]

Political action was the theme of the 1959 AFL-CIO convention that convened in San Francisco. In June, prior to the convention, Congress passed the Landrum-Griffin Act. Landrum-Griffin was the first major piece of labor legislation passed in the twelve years since Taft-Hartley. It was a strong labor reform bill that regulated the internal procedures and affairs of trade unions. The bill called for annual reports from unions to the Secretary of Labor; it regulated such internal matters as the election of officers and the relation of affiliates to their local unions; and it contained amendments to the National Labor Relations Act. The AFL-CIO felt the Act infringed upon the autonomy of trade unions and opposed it vigorously, but had lost the legislative battle. In his address that officially opened the 1959 convention, C. J. Haggerty, president of the California state AFL-CIO, indicated that a reevaluation of COPE would have a high priority on the convention's agenda, "We will have to do some revising of our usual techniques and tactics and procedures if we are to meet the present onslaught of the non-union and anti-union employers....We may have to revise our method of communication to our people....But I am sure that when this convention has arrived at its conclusion we will have the answer."[43]

The conclusion the convention reached was that COPE should continue to do what it had been doing, but only to do more of it. This followed from the AFL-CIO leadership's analysis of what had gone wrong in the battle over labor reform. The leadership argued that Landrum-Griffin was enacted not because labor was betrayed by the friends it had elected in 1958, but because there were not enough of them. In the crucial vote on labor reform legislation, 95 Democrats voted for the substitute Landrum-Griffin Bill over a measure supported by the AFL-CIO. Ninety-two of these Democrats were from Southern or Plains states. There were only three defections among the 174 Democratic congressmen from Northern or Western states. Of the 181 COPE endorsed congressmen elected in 1958, sixteen voted against the recommendation of the AFL-CIO. Fourteen of these renegades were Democrats, all of whom came from Southern or Plains states. COPE experienced only four defections from among the 52 first term congressmen it endorsed in 1958.[44]

Using this arithmetic, AFL-CIO leaders argued that the passage of Landrum-Griffin was the product of an unholy alliance between Republicans and Southern Democrats. Meany charged that Landrum-Griffin had passed because Republican congressmen exchanged votes to block civil rights legislation in return for cooperation from Southern Democrats in passing restrictive labor legislation.[45] Thus, labor leaders concluded that COPE's victory in 1958 had been a real one, only not sufficient to defeat the bipartisan conservative coalition that passed Landrum-Griffin. If COPE was guilty of anything in 1958, it was guilty of miscalculating the extent of its victory.

The Resolution on Political Activity that was passed at the convention called upon local central bodies and local unions to increase their register-and-vote activity; for affiliated unions to "assume their full share of organizational and moral responsibility" by meeting their financial obligation to COPE; and for more political education of the membership.[46] Leonard Woodcock from the Auto Workers rose to support the Resolution. He agreed with the leadership's position that Landrum-Griffin was the child of a cynical marriage between Southern Democrats and conservative Republicans in Congress. According to Woodcock, the vote on Landrum-Griffin indicated that the COPE program was basically sound only it needed to be pursued more vigorously.[47] Others, however, were not so sanguine. Michael Quill from the Transit Workers Union and R. G. Soderstrom (Illinois state AFL-

CIO) both urged the Executive Council to consider the formation of a labor party.[48]   But remarks similar to Woodcock's were in greater evidence in the discussion on political action than comments by those who dissented. Joseph Keenan, president of the IBEW, admonished the delegates for their lack of support of COPE. "Everyone sitting in this room, every executive officer, knows in his heart how much effort he has put forward for COPE. And I think the records will show that it is not in the majority. But this is the kind of crack in the jaw you need to get going."[49] Keenan argued that if COPE was to carry out the mandate of the convention it needed greater support from the affiliates. Another delegate agreed with Keenan's remark about the hidden benefits of a crack in the jaw.   Landrum-Griffin may have provided the labor movement the motivation it needed to take political action more seriously. According to AFL-CIO Vice President Joe Walsh, federal law that regulated the internal behavior of trade unions would now compel local union leaders to engage in political activity. Only by demonstrating their political strength could they be certain that the law would be administered favorably. The message on political action the delegates should take back to their locals was:

> You are not talking about the individual [candidate] anymore....You are talking about who sets your initiation fee. You are talking about how your finances should be handled. You are talking about the Constitution and by-laws of your unions....So let's get home to the members of our local unions that we are electing people who are going to write our constitutions and our by-laws and under federal law we are going to have to live with it.[50]

The convention ended with more attention devoted to political action than any previous AFL-CIO gathering, but no new strategies were drafted. The affiliated unions were once again urged to commit more resources to COPE and to place more pressure upon their local unions to comply with COPE's requests, just like they had been urged to do after the 1957 AFL-CIO convention. But no organizational changes were made to give COPE authority to ensure that the affiliated unions complied with the Resolution on Political Action the convention had just adopted. A resolution that would have strengthened state and local COPEs by mandating local union affiliation to state and local central bodies was voted down by the delegates.

Although no structural changes emerged from the convention that could strengthen COPE and mitigate its dependence on the affiliates, the passage of Landrum-Griffin did arouse the political sensibilities of the affiliated unions. The challenge Landrum-Griffin posed to their institutional autonomy awakened them to their need for stronger and more systematic political organization.

In 1960, five years after its birth, COPE finally became a national organization with COPE committees that operated in all 50 states. In addition, trade union support of COPE increased. COPE would no longer be sustained by unions from the old CIO and a handful of AFL unions like the ITU or IBEW. Now, for the first time in 1960, the building trades would participate in COPE's register-and-vote drive and contribute money and staff to COPE for use in the 1960 campaign. This new interest in COPE among the building trades was first previewed at the 51st Building and Construction Trades convention held just prior to the AFL-CIO convention in San Francisco. Speaking at the convention, McDevitt addressed himself to those unions who had not met their obligation to COPE because they did not see the value of political activity. "I am sure by this hour, for those who weren't convinced, that they must be convinced now, that the only hope for our situation is political education."[51] McDevitt's speech touched off a spontaneous collection for COPE to demonstrate building trades support. The convention then called for a "more effective program of accelerated and improved political action."[52]

In 1960, COPE also began to engage in voter aggregation activity on behalf of the Democratic party on a national scale. Following the AFL-CIO convention in San Francisco, Phil Weightman wrote a memo to McDevitt outlining the strategy COPE was to use in the 1960 campaign. Weightman proposed that COPE's 1960 registration drive be concentrated in fifteen states where large numbers of trade union members and minorities resided. Minority groups, Weightman felt, were as disappointed with the social and economic record of the Eighty-sixth Congress as labor was with its record on labor legislation. This made minority groups a fertile ground for political mobilization in the 1960 campaign. Moreover, blacks had shown that they were receptive to trade union appeals in the right-to-work referendums of 1958. Weightman recommended that local unions and local central body COPEs link up with interested groups in their area and make a community project out of registration. "The success of this program will be determined by the cooperation of our International unions and our State Central Bodies in giving us staff and support."[53]

In 1960, the AFL-CIO created a special fund to finance a registration drive to be targeted not only at union members but minorities as well. In this way it hoped to increase the turnout for Democratic party candidates. Following the passage of Landrum-Griffin, the AFL-CIO increasingly provided campaign assistance to the Democratic party because it identified the defense of its market strategy with the Party's political success.

COPE AND THE 1960 ELECTION

COPE's biweekly publication, *Memo From COPE*, opened the new year by announcing labor's theme for the 1960 campaign. "The challenge which labor faces at the polls this year...[is] voting out of office those politicians who want to put trade unionists in a strait jacket."[54] In January, 600 delegates to the AFL-CIO's Legislative Conference were regaled with the need to "get our people to register and vote." The conference spent more time trying to persuade delegates that the key to a sympathetic Congress was a strong COPE program in their local unions and communities than it did in its normal task of lobbying.[55] But labor was still stung by the passage of Landrum-Griffin. They continued to feel betrayed by the Democrats on Landrum-Griffin despite the analysis of the congressional vote presented at the last convention. George Harrison, President of the Railway Clerks and chair of the Labor Committee for every Democratic presidential candidate since Roosevelt, stated publicly that he did not believe labor would endorse a presidential candidate in 1960. Union officials were also noticeably absent from the Democratic party's presidential campaign kickoff dinner in February.[56]

Landrum-Griffin was the center of attention at COPE area conferences in 1960. At each conference, COPE spokesmen tried to impress the delegates that Landrum-Griffin meant the internal affairs of their local unions were now subject to political regulation. McDevitt then claimed that all of this could have been avoided if, initially, local leaders had given COPE the cooperation and support expected of them. McDevitt argued that the lack of cooperation COPE received from the local union leadership was the biggest problem that COPE encountered. At the COPE area conference in Durham, North Carolina, McDevitt complained, "We don't have any trouble in educating the rank and file member to the necessity of voting if we could reach him. But we can only reach the rank and file member through the union leaders."[57] According to McDevitt, many local unions simply had not established COPE committees to check registration, educate their members, or solicit contributions for COPE. All too often COPE literature remained in local union headquarters undistributed to the membership. Where local union COPE committees were established, they were only given *proforma* assistance and functioned only as registration deadlines or election day approached.

The fault, however, lay not entirely with the local union leadership but with the affiliated unions as well. At the COPE area conference in Philadelphia, McDevitt told the delegates that the affiliated unions were dragging their feet on political education. "This applies to some International Presidents who comprise the important AFL-CIO Committee [AFL-CIO Executive Council] which controls and is supposed to direct labor's political program."[58] According to McDevitt, COPE's organizational dependence on the affiliated unions for funds, staff, and contact with the membership inhibited COPE's effectiveness.

In August, McDevitt took his complaint about the lack of cooperation COPE received from the affiliates before the AFL-CIO Executive Council. He reminded council members that COPE was dependent upon the support it received from them. If they expected

COPE to mobilize the membership in the approaching election they "must decide here and now the extent of our interest in the 1960 campaign....Each COPE Area Director covers a vast territory. Each National WAD Director covers half the country. The Field Director is responsible for the Minority Program in all fifty states. Without the active enthusiasm and support of the International unions, COPE cannot be a real force, a respected force, in American life."[59]

McDevitt then outlined COPE's strategy for the 1960 election. Uppermost in his mind was defeat of the conservative coalition in Congress that had passed Landrum-Griffin. Two strategies were recommended for deposing this bipartisan coalition. One strategy called for COPE to concentrate its efforts outside the South in working class congressional districts represented by conservative Republicans. For example, Ohio's fourteenth district contained many union members who worked in the manufacturing plants and rubber mills of Akron, Ohio. This district was represented by William Ayers, a conservative Republican who had voted for Landrum-Griffin. The other strategy called for COPE to concentrate its efforts in the South and challenge the regular Democratic party organization in that region.

In fact, COPE was to attempt both a "Northern" and "Southern" strategy to break the hold of the conservative coalition on Congress. Chapter 5 shows that COPE was instrumental in financing civil rights organizations that attempted to register black voters in the South. These new voters could be used as shock troops to unseat Southern Democrats who voted against AFL-CIO recommendations in Congress. But a Southern strategy was longterm, and one in which COPE could only play a supporting role to civil rights organizations. In his Report to the COPE Administrative Committee [AFL-CIO Executive Council] McDevitt felt there was "little or no hope of increasing liberal Congressional representation from the South in 1960." For the immediate future, the 1960 election, McDevitt told the COPE Administrative Committee that the political solution to the conservative coalition had to come from Northern areas where the labor movement was well organized. But even here McDevitt admitted that "Without a liberal landslide in the North and West comparable to the election of 1936, there is little hope of electing enough liberals outside the South to defeat the coalition." Still, attention to these areas could expect to yield more dividends than if resources were directed elsewhere.[60]

Plans took shape to implement COPE's Northern strategy. COPE selected twelve states where it would concentrate its register-and-vote drive: California, Illinois, Indiana, Maryland, Michigan, Missouri, Minnesota, New Jersey, New York, Ohio, Pennsylvania, and Wisconsin. These states were chosen on the basis of two criteria. First, they contained more than two-thirds of all AFL-CIO members in the United States. Second, they were selected because each state contained large minority populations that COPE predicted would vote for liberal Democrats if they could be registered and brought to the polls to vote.

Within each state, urban areas were targeted for special attention on registration.

The 1960 registration drive was to be funded by a special voluntary assessment of $0.05 per member on affiliated unions. This assessment for the registration campaign was separate from the quota each union was supposed to contribute to COPE for the 1960 campaign. Direction over the campaign was removed from COPE and turned over to Carl McPeak, a troubleshooter from Meany's office. By placing direction of the registration campaign outside of COPE, Meany hoped to underscore its nonpartisan character and remove to the background AFL-CIO sponsorship of the project.[61]

Although COPE did not direct the registration campaign, COPE distributed money for registration work and its personnel helped direct the campaign in targeted states. Checks from COPE totaling more than $500,000 were made out to Non-Partisan Registration Committees in 28 states between September 1 and November 2, 1960. Eighty percent of this money went to the 12 states targeted for special attention on registration. The California State AFL-CIO received $50,000 from COPE for use in its registration campaign; Illinois was sent $45,000, with more than one-half of that stipulated for registration work in Cook County, and $5,300 for minority registration; $31,000 was sent to Indiana, with $9,000 of that targeted for East Chicago and Indianapolis; Michigan received $41,000, of which $4,500 was stipulated for minority registration within the state; Minnesota received $16,000; New York was sent $77,000 of which $12,000 was to be spent on minority registration; Pennsylvania was allocated $27,850; Wisconsin received $25,500; New Jersey was sent $21,000; Missouri received $15,500; Maryland was allocated $19,800; and Ohio was sent $51,000.[62]

Manpower for the campaign was pulled from COPE and other AFL-CIO departments including the Speaker's Bureau, Community Services, the AFL-CIO regional staff, and the entire staff from the Department of Organization. On September 9, McDevitt sent a letter to all of the affiliated unions requesting the services of as many staff representatives and business agents as they could spare. He assured them that since any staff released to COPE would work on the registration campaign it was legal for the unions to continue to pay their staff out of their own general funds.

In order to broaden participation in the campaign, local unions were instructed to join with interested local groups to form Non-Partisan Registration Committees. Wherever possible, people from outside of organized labor were to be recruited to serve as officers on these committees. In California, for example, registration committees appeared in every city throughout the state. The committees hired registrars and offered $0.15 to $0.25 for every name they filed with the Board of Elections. In minority districts, California Labor COPE gave money to black and Chicano organizations so they could employ deputized registrars to turn in names to the Board of Elections. Vice

President of California Labor COPE, C. A. Green, reported to COPE Deputy Director Al Barkan in Washington that, "In every key area where there is a substantial number of unregistered minority group individuals we are heavily subsidizing both the N.A.A.C.P. and the C.S.O."[63]

In Baltimore the registration drive was particularly well organized. The officers of the Maryland AFL-CIO and the Baltimore AFL-CIO council founded the Baltimore Non-Partisan Registration Committee. Dominic Fornaro, Vice-Chairman of Baltimore Labor COPE was made chairman and Claude Callegary, a lawyer, was appointed treasurer. In September, the committee distributed 24,000 leaflets and provided buses to transport people from their homes to the registration offices and back. Because of the unexpected large turnout for registration in Baltimore the Board of Elections had to move their registration facilities to the War Memorial Building to accommodate the crowds. Office space for the committee was furnished by Meat Cutters Local 117, Steelworker locals provided canvassers, ILGWU members made phone calls, the Hod Carriers provided clerical assistance, and Transit Workers drove people to the Board of Elections. Staff representatives from the Auto Workers, Machinists, Woodworkers Union, and the Steelworkers worked closely with the committee. After a three-week effort, the committee reported that 51,734 new registrants were filed to vote, with 75 percent of them registering as Democrats.[64]

COPE estimated that 9,100 workers took part in the registration campaign. In addition, COPE produced more registration material in all fields of communication than were ever produced by any previous labor effort.[65] COPE estimated at the conclusion of its registration drive that it had helped qualify 1,500,000 people to vote.

Once registration deadlines in the states had passed, COPE began to organize campaigns on behalf of endorsed candidates. The 1960 COPE campaign is noteworthy only because of the participation of the building trades in it. In previous campaigns, the building trades balked at collecting money for COPE, distributing COPE literature, or coordinating their activities through state and local COPEs. But in 1960, C. J. Haggerty replaced Richard Gray as President of the AFL-CIO Building and Construction Trades Department. Haggerty had been a firm supporter of COPE activities while serving as President of the California state AFL-CIO while Gray had never reconciled himself to the merger. The passage of the Landrum-Griffin Act and the nomination of an Irish Catholic as the Democratic party's presidential candidate also sparked interest in COPE among the building trades. In August, the Building and Construction Trades Bulletin carried an article entitled "The Need for Union Members to Register and Vote." The article detailed an eight-step program a local union could follow to qualify union members to vote. It reminded its readers that the value of a strong COPE program had proven itself in the defeat of right-to-work amendments in Ohio and California in 1958.[66] In 1960, the Lathers Union, Plumbers, IBEW, Asbestos Workers, and Operating Engineers all met or surpassed their

COPE quota of voluntary contributions from the membership.

The 1960 "dollar drive" was COPE's most successful to date. In 1960 COPE collected 56.4 percent of its quota from the affiliates based upon $1.00 from 25 percent of a union's membership. This was almost ten percent better than COPE did financially in 1956. A comparison of the contributions to COPE from individual unions will permit us to analyze interunion variations in COPE support.[67]

TABLE 4-1:   SCHEDULE OF CONTRIBUTIONS TO COPE, 1960

Union	Political Fund	Educational Fund	% of Quota Achieved
Aluminum Workers	560.00	500.00	51.9
Asbestos Workers	2,258.00	60.00	185.4
Auto Workers	97,041.67	50,000.00	116.6
Allied Workers	5,190.58	-	59.2
Bakery & Confectionery	2,701.30	-	33.1
Barbers	1,268.50	17.00	14.1
Boilermakers	-	-	-
Bookbinders	1,534.50	51.00	22.4
Brewery Workers	8,299.55	-	147.5
Bricklayers	4,412.57	40.00	29.6
Brick & Clay	352.80	760.00	34.4
Bridge & Structural	2,540.05	37.00	14.7
Broadcast Employees	5,528.50	425.00	181.6
Building Service	2,939.00	55,044.00	29.1
Cement, Lime & Gypsum	1,499.70	55.00	35.2
Chemical Workers	3,028.39	5,279.61	101.7
Cigarmakers	45.60	350.00	53.3
Clothing Workers	20,000.00	6,500.00	73.6
CWA	15,023.81	12,313.91	107.4
Coopers	2.00	400.00	94.6
Distillery Workers	5,184.00	-	126.5
Doll & Toy Workers	474.00	-	19.9
IUE	2,000.00	7,500.00	27.1
Electrical Workers	36,691.10	221.88	59.1
Elevator Construction	1,854.00	-	146.0
Engineers, Operating	19,909.00	5,000.00	73.8
Engineers, Tech.	445.50	21.00	29.1
Engravers, Photo	2,732.82	-	138.4
Fire Fighters	514.49	555.00	11.0
Flight Engineers	-	-	-

TABLE 4-1: Continued

Union	Political Fund	Educational Fund	% of Quota Achieved
Furniture Workers	2,858.35	-	62.8
ILGWU	15,000.00	-	33.0
Glass Bottle Blowers	2,000.00	4,585.00	100.1
Glass & Ceramic	7,267.11	4,500.00	230.5
Glass Workers, Flint	139.00	5,000.00	138.4
Glove Workers	-	-	-
Granite Cutters	-	-	-
Government Employees	127.00	39.00	2.2
Hatters	4,000.00	-	100.0
Hod Carriers	1,523.50	80.00	3.2
Horse Shoers	80.00	-	228.6
Hosiery Workers	427.25	263.00	100.4
Hotel & Restaurant	11,124.10	50.00	29.8
Insurance Workers	3,175.00	-	117.6
Jewelry Workers	1,133.25	100.00	91.7
Lathers	2,324.50	1,160.00	116.5
Laundry Workers	2,340.00	35.00	112.0
Leather Goods	105.00	-	2.8
Leather Workers	-	-	-
Machinists	2,930.00	-	3.0
Marble Polishers	261.00	10.00	27.1
Marine & Shipbuilding	161.00	3,195.00	105.0
Marine Engineers	-	-	-
Maritime Union	4,750.00	-	100.0
Meat Cutters	9,795.54	1,010.00	26.6
Mechanics Educ. Society	-	-	-
Metal Workers, Sheet	2,627.00	6,883.00	101.4
Milkers, Grain	105.00	-	2.8
Musicians	731.00	15,020.00	51.7
Newspaper Guild	1,172.66	1,705.00	101.5
Office Employees	1,951.29	-	32.0
Oil, Chemical & Atomic	19,142.15	122.50	101.9
Packinghouse Workers	10,782.09	-	108.1
Painters	5,643.00	7,639.00	63.9
Papermakers & Paperworkers	9,085.54	5,609.00	95.7
Plasterers	2,330.00	6,764.00	107.0
Plate Printers	-	100.00	100.00
Plumbers	9,597.00	1,310.00	99.6

TABLE 4-1: Continued

Union	Political Fund	Educational Fund	% of Quota Achieved
Polishers Metal	37.00	-	2.3
Porters, Sleeping Car	-	-	-
Printing Pressmen	3,890.00	60.00	32.1
Pulp, Sulphite	9,215.01	1,505.00	63.0
Radio Assistant	197.50	-	100.0
Retail Clerks	10,076.00	-	24.6
Rwy Emps, Street & Elec.	9,481.00	200.00	69.5
RWDSW	13,571.00	-	101.7
Roofers	146.00	1,000.00	44.1
Rubber Workers	26,342.38	-	126.4
Shoe Workers, United	4,747.00	2,350.75	115.0
Stage Employees	8,885.00	22.00	141.3
State, Co. & Municipal	2,954.90	3,856.35	30.0
Steel Workers	-	65,380.00	100.0
Stereotypers	3,762.75	-	254.2
Stone & Allied Workers	366.50	286.32	42.8
Stove Mounters	151.00	100.00	26.4
Teachers	1,367.75	262.50	24.7
Telegraphers, Comm.	2,415.80	-	72.3
Textile Workers, United	446.00	-	10.0
Textile Workers, Union	3,750.00	15,000.00	100.0
Tobacco Workers	448.00	795.50	36.9
Transport Service	168.00	-	44.8
Transport Workers	5,000.00	5,000.00	100.0
Typographical Union	18,572.97	-	185.9
Upholsterers	3,935.25	10.00	71.2
Utility Workers	649.00	516.00	58.7
Woodworkers	1,642.70	3,184.00	63.9
Federal Labor Unions	1,520.40	2,500.00	11.4
Government Workers:			
Clerks, Post Office	6.00	-	.1
Letter Carriers	2.50	-	-
Post Office Motor Vehicle	-	-	-
Transport Service Mail	-	-	-
Postal Transport, Nat'l.	-	-	-
Siderographers	6.00	-	100.0
Special Delivery Mssngrs	-	-	-

TABLE 4-1: Continued

Union	Political Fund	Educational Fund	% of Quota Achieved
Railway League:			
Carmen, Railway	45.00	-	.4
Clerks, Railway	63.00	-	.2
Firemen, Locomotive	213.00	1,000.00	20.1
Firemen, Oilers	408.00	-	6.5
Maintenance of Way	-	-	-
Railway Patrol	-	-	-
Railway Supervisors	-	-	-
Miscellaneous:			
Bldg. & Constr. Trades	1,051.85	25.00	-
Central Labor Union	768.50	150.00	-
State AFL-CIOs	-	-	-
State & Local COPEs	6,029.00	3,600.00	-
WADs	559.00	25.00	-
Staff	7,915.00	-	-
Misc. Individuals	22,344.79	20,500.00	-
Contributions From Local Unions:			
Actors	-	-	-
Agricultural Workers	-	-	-
Air Line Dispatchers	-	-	-
Air Line Pilot	-	-	-
Bill Posters	20.00	-	-
Boot & Shoe	-	-	10.0
Broom & Whist Makers	-	-	-
Carpenters	2,830.00	25.00	3.0
Garment Workers United	30.50	-	81.5
Glass Cutters	163.00	-	-
Longshoreman	18.00	-	16.8
Masters, Mates	200.00	-	8.4
Molders	557.50	7.50	2.8
Pattern Makers	39.00	-	41.5
Potters	295.50	1,000.00	-
Radio & TV	-	-	-
Seafarers	281.00	2.00	4.4
Stonecutters	-	-	-

In his case studies, Greenstone found that former CIO unions offered more assistance to COPE than did unions from the old AFL. Our figures support this finding. Even as late as 1960, unions from the old CIO carried an unfair burden of COPE's financial support. Former CIO unions—including those CIO unions who had merged with their AFL counterparts since 1955—accounted for one-half of the money COPE received in voluntary contributions from the membership and two-thirds of the money donated to COPE's Educational Fund. Collectively, these unions met 98 percent of their financial obligation to COPE, while the rest of the unions only met 33 percent of their COPE quota.

Former CIO unions were more likely to meet their quota for several reasons. First, CIO unions were better prepared organizationally and psychologically to contribute money for political work. PAC had been a much more dynamic organization than LLPE. The greater experience of CIO unions in collecting money for political activity accounts for part of the difference.

Another reason why CIO unions were better at collecting money for COPE has to do with the composition of their membership. Unskilled workers have a greater stake in national economic policy than skilled workers. They are more vulnerable to the vicissitudes of macroeconomic policy than skilled workers who work in more specialized product and labor markets.

Finally, CIO leaders could still recall the role public policy played in helping to establish their unions. These unions owed a debt to the Wagner Act that became part of their tradition and history. This made CIO unions more sensitive to the services political action could provide trade unionism than AFL unions.

As much as the data tend to corroborate Greenstone's finding that COPE received more support from former CIO unions, the figures do not support this conclusion unambiguously. While former CIO unions were more likely to contribute to COPE, the Electrical Workers Union and the Stone and Allied Products Union—both former CIO unions—only met 27.1 percent and 42 percent of their quotas respectively. In comparison, old craft unions from the AFL like the Typeographers or Flint Glass Workers union—or even representatives from the building trades like the Lathers or the Elevator Construction Workers unions—exceeded their quotas. Infrastructural factors, such as the skill level of the membership, only provide a rough guide to the level of compensation COPE can expect to receive from a union. If the nature of work in an industry explained the amount of money COPE received, then we would expect to find unions in identical trades with similar rates of compensation. But this is not the case. Unions with overlapping jurisdictions like the Maritime Union (100 percent) and the Seafarers Union (4.4 percent), or the Retail and Wholesale Workers (101 percent) and the Retail Clerks Union (24.5 percent), were at opposite ends of the spectrum when it came to financial support of COPE.

One might also suspect that unions that ran their own political organizations parallel to COPE would be poor contributors. They would divert funds which might have gone to COPE into their own political organizations. But, again, this is not the case. While the Machinists (3.0 percent) and the ILGWU (33 percent) both ran their own political organizations parallel to COPE and were poor contributors, the Hatters (100 percent) and the Glass Bottle Blowers unions (101 percent) also ran internal political programs and met their quota.

The variability among our figures suggests that an important factor determining the level of compensation COPE receives from a union is the attitude of the affiliated union leadership towards COPE. The history of the Carpenters Union's relationship with COPE provides a good example of how the disposition of the leadership affects the level of support that COPE receives from a union.

Between 1952 and 1976 Maurice Hutcheson was president of the Brotherhood of Carpenters. Hutcheson was a Republican who frequently disagreed with AFL-CIO policy positions and COPE endorsements. As a result, his union rarely cooperated with COPE, either by donating money or lending staff for use in registration campaigns. When Hutcheson retired in 1972 he was replaced by William Sidell. Sidell was more sympathetic to COPE than Hutcheson and consequently the cooperation of the Carpenters with COPE increased. For the 17 years under the merger that Hutcheson was president his union contributed to COPE only once (1970). But beginning in 1972 when Sidell became president, the Carpenters contributed $50,000 or more to COPE for every year under his tenure (except 1976).[68]

Greenstone also uncovered evidence that leadership factors were more important than intrastructural characteristics in explaining interunion variations in COPE support. Discussing activity in one IBEW local where the local manager was committed to political action, he writes, "Indeed there appears to be a much closer relationship in Local 11 between union activity and political activism than in many industrial unions where the local officers were frequently too busy for much campaign work."[69]

In conclusion, where the president of an affiliate believes that COPE provides a service to his union or trade unionism in general, that union is likely to be a large contributor regardless of its composition. Where the leadership is in political disagreement with COPE, prefers to act independently, or is indifferent to political action, COPE does not receive much support from that union regardless of whether the membership is skilled or unskilled.

Before turning to how COPE fared in the 1960 election, how COPE spent the money it collected from the affiliates will be examined.[70]

TABLE 4-2:   SCHEDULE OF SPECIAL ALLOCATIONS, JANUARY 1-
NOVEMBER 30, 1960

State	Political Fund	Educational Fund
ALASKA		
Alaska State COPE	$4,000.00	$2,000.00
ARIZONA		
Arizona State COPE	1,500.00	
ARKANSAS		
Arkansas State COPE	1,000.00	
CALIFORNIA		
California State COPE	10,500.00	15,000.00
Regis. Drive, L.A. Area		7,500.00
COLORADO		
Colorado State COPE	17,000.00	
CONNECTICUT		
Connecticut State COPE	13,000.00	7,000.00
Connecticut State COPE		5,000.00
DELAWARE		
Delaware State COPE	2,000.00	5,000.00
FLORIDA		
Florida State COPE (m.g.)		500.00
GEORGIA		
Georgia State COPE	7,000.00	
HAWAII		
Hawaii State COPE (m.g.)		3,749.94
Hawaii State COPE	2,000.00	1,000.00
IDAHO		
Idaho State COPE (m.g.)		1,666.64
Idaho State COPE	18,000.00	4,000.00

TABLE 4-2:   Continued

State	Political Fund	Educational Fund
ILLINOIS		
Illinois State COPE	12,000.00	
Cook County COPE	13,800.00	11,500.00
Citizens for Douglas	10,000.00	
INDIANA		
Indiana State COPE	17,000.00	
IOWA		
Iowa State COPE	26,200.00	13,500.00
KANSAS		
Kansas State COPE	22,000.00	5,000.00
KENTUCKY		
Kentucky State COPE	7,000.00	
LOUISIANA		
Louisiana State COPE	9,000.00	12,500.00
MAINE		
Maine State COPE	13,000.00	17,500.00
MARYLAND		
Maryland State COPE	13,750.00	2,500.00
Friedel for Congress Comm.	7,030.00	
MASSACHUSETTS		
Massachusetts State COPE	15,500.00	5,000.00
MICHIGAN		
Michigan State COPE	30,000.00	5,000.00
MINNESOTA		
Minnesota State COPE	30,500.00	19,500.00
MISSOURI		
Missouri State COPE	23,500.00	100.00
Public Printer (Carnahan)	969.72	

TABLE 4-2:   Continued

State	Political Fund	Educational Fund
MONTANA		
Montana State COPE	11,250.00	22,250.00
D.C. Comm. for Metcalf	5,000.00	
NEBRASKA		
Nebraska State COPE	10,000.00	7,500.00
NEVADA		
Nevada State COPE	3,360.00	5,500.00
NEW HAMPSHIRE		
New Hampshire State COPE	1,000.00	
NEW JERSEY		
New Jesey State Fed. & I.U.C.	10,000.00	16,000.00
Essex-West Hudson COPE		2,000.00
NEW MEXICO		
New Mexico State COPE	14,000.00	1,500.00
NEW YORK		
New York State COPE	15,000.00	3,500.00
New York City COPE	2,500.00	
Public Printer (Santangelo)		225.92
NORTH CAROLINA		
North Carolina State COPE	14,000.00	10,000.00
Simpkins for Cong. Comm.	950.00	
NORTH DAKOTA		
North Dakota State COPE	11,000.00	14,000.00
OHIO		
Ohio State COPE	20,000.00	3,000.00
OKLAHOMA		
Oklahoma State COPE	8,000.00	1,500.00

TABLE 4-2:   Continued

State	Political Fund	Educational Fund
OREGON		
Oregon State COPE	10,000.00	12,000.00
PENNSYLVANIA		
Lycoming County COPE (17 CD)	2,500.00	2,000.00
Mifflin County COPE (18 CD)	1,000.00	2,000.00
Pennsylvania State COPE	20,000.00	5,000.00
Philadelphia, Erie and Bucks County COPE	1,000.00	1,900.00
Pittsburg C.L.U. and I.U.C.		10,000.00
RHODE ISLAND		
Rhode Island State COPE	6,000.00	15,000.00
SOUTH CAROLINA		
South Carolina State COPE		2,000.00
SOUTH DAKOTA		
South Dakota State COPE	18,000.00	14,285.93
TENNESSEE		
Tennessee State COPE	17,814.03	8,000.00
Friends of Kefauver	100.00	
Kefauver for Senate Comm.	10,000.00	
TEXAS		
Texas State COPE	15,000.00	10,000.00
UTAH		
Utah State COPE	4,000.00	8,000.00
VERMONT		
Vermont State COPE	2,000.00	7,600.00
VIRGINIA		
Virginia State COPE	4,000.00	1,500.00
WASHINGTON		
Washington State COPE	5,000.00	3,000.00

TABLE 4-2: Continued

State	Political Fund	Educational Fund
WEST VIRGINIA		
West Virginia State COPE	11,200.00	25,000.00
WISCONSIN		
Wisconsin State COPE	22,000.00	17,067.91
WYOMING		
Wyoming State COPE	11,000.00	9,999.96

Some candidates for the House and Senate like Estes Kefauver, Paul Douglas, and Lee Metcalf received contributions directly from COPE. But more than 97 percent of national COPE's disbursements went to the state AFL-CIOs.

The following factors are taken into account by COPE in distributing its money among the state organizations.

First, national COPE distributes its money to states where candidates with prolabor records are running for reelection. In 1960 Minnesota state COPE received the second highest amount of money that COPE distributed in order to help the state council support Hubert Humphrey's reelection bid.

COPE also considers whether a state organization has developed a COPE program worthy enough to justify an investment. Lethargic or indifferent state organizations that never made an effort to develop their COPE programs are passed over. Here, the reports from COPE's area directors are important in informing COPE's leadership in Washington, D.C., which states are worthy of financial support.[71]

A third factor COPE considers are the requests of affiliated unions who are large contributors to COPE. State organizations that are identified with unions that are large contributors—as the Michigan state AFL-CIO is linked with the Auto Workers and the Pennsylvania state AFL-CIO is identified with the Steelworkers—are sent large allotments. This is meant to reward affiliated unions for their COPE support. It is also not unusual for COPE to contribute money directly to a particular candidate at the request of an affiliate who is a large contributor.[72]

Finally, COPE applies a compensating strategy in its allocations to the state organizations. COPE distributes money to state organizations where it is interested in the outcome of a race, but the state organization is not able to provide the necessary assistance to favored candidates due to size restrictions. Nineteen states participated in a matching grants program that COPE set up in 1960 to help state organizations that have few members cover their political activity expenses. Two of these states, South Dakota and Montana, received compensation from COPE over and above their matching grant. In each case, COPE saw the chance of winning a closely contested seat but felt the state organization was not strong enough to bring the seat into labor's column without further financial assistance from the national office. In the case of South Dakota, a sizable contribution to the state COPE might enable the state labor organization to provide the difference for George McGovern in his Senate race against Karl Mundt. Mundt had consistently voted against labor's recommendations while in Congress.

In Montana assistance to the state COPE could help save Senator James Murray's seat for labor. Murray was retiring in 1960 and had been a solid labor supporter while in the Senate. Lee Metcalf was running for the seat Murray had last won in 1954 by only .04 percent of the vote. Thus, through its allocations, COPE tries to compensate for the weakness of COPE programs due to size restrictions in states where a close election vital to labor's interests is forecast.

COPE viewed the 1960 election results with mixed feelings. It was unable to depose the conservative coalition in Congress. But it was the presidential results that drew everyone's attention. Republican party strategists and the AFL-CIO both pointed to the union's registration drive as a major factor that contributed to Senator John F. Kennedy's victory. The defeated Republican candidate, Richard Nixon, declared, "Look at this close election and you can see that it was the work of the unions that made the difference."[73] Kennedy carried every major industrial state, except California and Ohio, due to the large pluralities he was able to win in urban areas where COPE had concentrated its registration drive. In its analysis of the presidential returns, the COPE research department found "Kennedy owed his victory to enormous Democratic margins in industrial areas and record breaking majorities in Negro wards and precincts." Labor wards in San Francisco (wards 20, 23, and 24) voted 2-to-1 for Kennedy, providing a margin of 50,000 votes out of 137,000 from these wards. Returns from labor wards in Bridgeport, Hartford, and New Haven showed Kennedy getting better than 2-to-1 of the vote, with black wards reporting even greater support. In Bridgeport the total vote almost doubled that of 1956 with almost all of the new voters voting Democratic. In Philadelphia Kennedy received the largest plurality any candidate ever received for any office in the history of the city. In Chicago labor wards voted 83.6 percent for Kennedy compared to only 67.4 percent for Stevenson in 1956. Similar 15 percent increases in the Democratic presidential vote over the 1956 results also occurred in labor wards in Pittsburg, Baltimore, and Milwaukee.[74] This led many columnists and Republican party campaign workers to credit COPE with Kennedy's victory.[75]

McDevitt did nothing to dispel this idea. He told the AFL-CIO

Executive Council after the election, "the efforts of national, state, and local COPEs contributed substantially to the victory of the Kennedy-Johnson ticket and a majority of the liberal U.S. Senators and Representatives. Indeed, in many cases it was THE deciding factor." McDevitt reminded the AFL-CIO Executive Council that Kennedy received a bare majority of 113,000 votes out of more than 68 million cast. With so close a margin "there is no question that COPE's registration activities throughout the country together with the AFL-CIO's 'crash' registration program was the straw which broke the camel's back."

McDevitt also reported that COPE's registration work among minorities had paid off handsomely. Record-breaking Democratic majorities among black and Hispanic voters helped account for the huge Democratic margins from urban areas. The plurality for Kennedy was so great from Philadelphia, Pittsburg, Baltimore, St. Louis, and Detroit that it was enough to carry the state for Kennedy in each instance. Blacks gave Kennedy the highest average support of any ethnic group. According to McDevitt they were responsible for carrying the five states he had designated as "must states if Kennedy was to win: New York, Michigan, New Jersey, Illinois, and Pennsylvania....In short, we can safely say that the Negro vote firmly aligned itself with organized labor....We were more than repaid for our efforts."[76]

In later years COPE would build upon this initial success in mobilizing the Democratic party constituency.

CONCLUSION

This chapter has examined the early years of COPE from 1956 to 1960. The period is noteworthy for COPE's organizational development and for COPE's voter-aggregation activity on behalf of the Democratic party.

Between 1956 and 1960 the organizational structure of COPE was set into place. After an inauspicious start, state COPEs—often with full-time COPE Directors—were operative in every state by 1960. However, the establishment of local COPEs and local union COPE committees did not proceed as quickly. Here, at the most critical levels, COPE still often lacked adequate organization. Only threats to union security—as appeared in 1958—could generate responses from these quarters. Once these threats were removed, organization at the local central body and local union levels dissipated.

Organizational maturity is also evident in the wider range of unions COPE received support from between 1956 and 1960. Financial support of COPE became more evenly distributed among the affiliates, although CIO unions still evinced greater support of COPE than former AFL unions.

Finally, in this chapter we found that institutional, rather than broad policy concerns, account for why the union-party linkage grew progressively stronger following merger. The politicization of labor relations, first appearing in the guise of right-to-work referendums and then the Landrum-Griffin Act, deepened and extended the trend toward the politicization of labor relations set in motion by the New Deal. In order to protect the collective bargaining and institutional interests of the affiliated unions, COPE aggregated voters outside the AFL-CIO membership into the Party. Instead of serving as a flow channel for the welfare state demands of the membership, COPE served the interests of the affiliated and local union leadership in institutional preservation. Only on this basis could COPE obtain their cooperation and support upon which the success of the whole enterprise depended.

NOTES

1. Interview with Henry Murray, COPE area director for New England, April 22, 1979, New Haven, Conn.

2. Interview with Henry Murray, *op. cit.*, and interview with Dan Powell, COPE area director for the Deep South, January 23, 1981, Memphis, Tenn. Both Murray and Powell had worked for PAC before joining COPE.

3. Interview with Al Barkan, Director of COPE, November 22, 1979, Washington, D.C.

4. "Speech at Oberlin" in Jack Kroll Papers, Box 5; Folder "Speeches, Writings, and Related Material, 1956," Library of Congress, Manuscripts Division, Washington, D.C.

5. Pulp, Paper and Sulphite Workers Convention Proceedings, 1956, 54.

6. "COPE Report to the AFL-CIO Executive Council" in Jack Kroll Papers, Box 5; Folder, "Speeches, Writings and Related Material, 1956."

7. James L. McDevitt and Jack Kroll, "Give COPE Your Support," *American Federationist* (May 1956): 10.

8. See reports of the COPE Research Department, Lot 1, Box 5; Folder 32, in George Meany Memorial Archives, Silver Springs, Maryland.

9. "How Unions Came Out in the Election," *U.S. News and World Report* (November 16, 1956): 101-11.

10. "Labor," *Fortune* (November 1956): 231.

11. "Jack Kroll and Jim McDevitt to all former AFL Local Unions" in Dan Powell Papers, Folder 77, Southern History Collection, Library of the University of North Carolina, Chapel Hill, N.C.

12. "Preliminary Analysis of the 1956 National Elections" in Jack Kroll Papers, Box 5; Folder, "Speeches, Writings and Related Materials, 1956."

13. Ibid.

14. Ibid.

15. Industrial Unions Department Convention Proceedings, 1957, 74.

16. "Comparisons of Campaigns: 1956-1958-1960" in possession of author.

17. Industrial Unions Department Convention Proceedings, 1957, 74.

18. "Report of the COPE Director to the COPE Administrative Committee," in COPE Research Department files, Lot 1, Box 3; Folder 32.

19. Ibid.

20. James L. McDevitt, "The People Are Deeply Concerned" *American Federationist* (August 1958): 11-13.

21. "Labor Goes on the Political Defensive," *Business Week* (October 18, 1958): 147.

22. *Wall Street Journal*, (November 7, 1958).

23. "Report of the COPE Area Conference in Atlanta, Ga., May, 1958," in Claude Ramsey Papers, Box 13; Folder, "6th District COPE," Southern Labor Archives, Georgia State University, Atlanta, Georgia.

24. "What Happened in the Election," *U.S. News and World Report* (November 14, 1958): 47.

25. Totten J. Anderson, "The 1958 Election in California," *Western Political Quarterly* (March 1959): 289-90. See also Gilbert Gall, "Sterile Combat: Labor, Politics, and Right-to-Work," (Ph.D., Wayne State University, 1984), 151-58.

26. Lester Velie, *Labor, U.S.A.* (New York: Harper and Row, 1959), 250-55; Gall, *op. cit.,* 164.

27. California Labor COPE Pre-Primary Convention Proceedings, 1962, 9.

28. Ibid., 9.

29. "'Why I Won'-'Why I Lost,'" *U.S. News and World Report,* (November 14, 1958): 106.

30. Glenn W. Miller and Stephen B. Ware, "Organized Labor in the Political Process: A Case Study of the Right-to-Work Campaign in Ohio," *Labor History* (Winter 1963): 54.

31. Ibid., 54.

32. Philip M. Weightman to Jim McDevitt (December 1, 1958) in Philip M. Weightman Collection, Box 7; Folder "Right-to-Work," Robert F. Wagner Labor Archives, New York University, N.Y.

33. Ibid.

34. Miller and Ware, 67.

35. Jack Kroll to Jim McDevitt in Jack Kroll Papers, Box 5; Folder, "Correspondence, 1960."

36. "Field Report," Dan Powell to Jim McDevitt (November 2, 1958) in Dan Powell Papers, Folder 77.

37. "Field Report," Dan Powell to Jim McDevitt (October 6, 1958) in Dan Powell Papers, Folder 77.

38. "What Happened in the Election," *U.S. News and World Report* (November 14, 1958): 47.

39. Gary Fink (ed.), *AFL-CIO Executive Council Statements and Reports, 1965-1975,* Vol. 1 (Westport, Conn.: Greenwood Press, 1977), 339.

40. "George Meany, "Don't Force American Labor to Start A Political Party," *Commercial and Financial Chronicle* (January 15, 1959): 109.

41. James McDevitt, "The People Do Alright," *American Federationist* (December 1958): 10-11.

42. *AFL-CIO News* (August 29, 1959).

43. AFL-CIO Convention Proceedings, 1959, Vol. I, 5-6.

44. Carl MacAdams, *Power and Politics in Labor Legislation* (New York: Columbia University Press, 1974), 202-4.

45. AFL-CIO Convention Proceedings, 1959, Vol. I, 375.

46. Ibid., 374.

47. Ibid., 381.

48. Ibid., 384.

49. Ibid., 390.

50. Ibid., 389-91.

51. Building and Construction Trades Convention Proceedings, 1959, 158.

52. Ibid., 153.

53. "Minorities Report for 1959," in Philip Weightman Collection, Folder "COPE-National."

54. *Memo From Cope* (January, 1960).

55. *AFL-CIO News* (January 16, 1960).

56. *Wall Street Journal* (February 11, 1960).

57. *Durham Labor Journal* (February 19, 1960), in COPE Research Department files, Lot 1, Box 3; Folder 28.

58. *New Jersey Labor Journal* (March, 1960), in COPE Research Department files, Lot 1, Box 3; Folder 28.

59. "Report of the National Director" (August 16, 1960), in COPE Research Department files, Lot 1, Box 3; Folder 28.

60. Ibid.

61. Reports on the registration campaign can be found in the *New York Times* (August 18, 1960); and "Unions Enter Political Arena with Drive to Get Out the Vote," *Business Week* (August 27, 1960): 108-13.

62.   "Schedule of Special Allocations" in possession of author.

63.   C. A. Green to Al Barkan (September 16, 1960), in Philip Weightman Collection, Box 5; Folder "Al Barkan."

64.   Dominic Fornaro to Al Barkan (October 17, 1960), in Philip Weightman Collection, Box 5; Folder "Al Barkan."

65.   Henry Zon to James L. McDevitt (November 22, 1960), in Philip Weightman Collection, Box 6; Folder "Registration Program (1960) Publicity."

66.   "The Need for Union Members to Register and Vote," the *Building and Construction Trades Bulletin* (August 16, 1960).

67.   "Schedule of Contributions to COPE, 1960," in possession of author.

68.   "Contributions, Gifts, and Grants," *Labor Organizations Annual Report*, Department of Labor, Form L-M II, Schedule 12, 1980.

69.   J. David Greenstone, *Labor in American Politics*, 2nd edition (Chicago: University of Chicago Press, 1977), 206.

70.   "COPE Schedule of Allocations, 1960" in possession of author.

71.   Interview with Dan Powell, *op. cit.*

72.   Ibid.

73.   "Inside Story: Why It Wasn't Nixon," *U.S. News and World Report* (January 30, 1961): 40-41.

74.   "The 1960 Election," by the COPE Research Department in Philip Weightman Collection, Box 6; Folder "1960 Election Statistics and Reports."

75.   For such analyses see *New York Times* (November 11, 1960); and *Washington Daily News* (November 10, 1960).

76.   "National Director's Report to the COPE Administrative Committee," in COPE Research Department files, Lot 1, Box 3; Folder 31.

5. *From Victory to Defeat*

Between 1960 and 1967 COPE consciously identified its constituency beyond the union membership and sought to recruit minorities into the Democratic party. But the more COPE attempted to mobilize the wider Democratic party coalition the more trouble it had in gaining the cooperation and support of secondary labor leaders. Local union leaders had little interest in aggregating voters outside the union membership into the Party. In lieu of direct threats to their collective bargaining interests, the fortunes of the Democratic party were of only limited concern to them. In addition, as long as the labor movement pursued a market strategy, the membership could not build up a stake in social welfare programs such that they would pressure their leaders to defend such programs politically: that is, to the point of keeping Democrats in office. Finally, racism within the rank and file paralyzed local union leaders and prevented them from participating in COPE's partisan strategy. Unable to depend on the support of secondary labor leaders, COPE covertly implemented its partisan strategy by working through organizations outside the labor movement, particularly civil rights organizations, to broaden support for the Democratic party.

Going around the local union leadership was, however, not without its consequences. The costs of this tactical decision were thrown into sharp relief by the 1966 congressional elections. In these

---

*Portions of this chapter appeared originally in my article "Labor and the 1966 Elections," *Labor History*, Vol. 30, Winter 1988-89. The author gratefully acknowledges the permission of The Tamiment Institute, which publishes *Labor History*, to use this material.

elections, the membership repudiated the most liberal and sympathetic Congress the AFL-CIO had ever encountered, one that was responsible for passing legislation the unions had sought for over twenty years. In response to this sensational defeat COPE commissioned John Kraft Inc. to conduct a poll on the political attitudes of union members. The poll discovered that demographic changes had reoriented the political concerns of the membership. Consumer-community issues of neighborhood preservation, lower taxes, and zoning regulations were found to be of more vital interest to workers than traditional issues such as improving workman's compensation and unemployment insurance, or issues of union security.

This chapter is organized into two sections. The first section reviews the organizational problems COPE continued to experience in the 1960s. The second section details COPE's role in the rise and fall of the liberal Democratic coalition. It examines the support COPE gave to civil rights organizations in the South and the problems it encountered in this regard. It then describes COPE's activity in the 1964 and 1966 elections and the thorough examination COPE received following the crushing defeat of COPE-endorsed candidates in the 1966 elections.

COPE'S DISORGANIZATION

McDevitt was rightfully proud of the results from COPE's 1960 registration campaign. However, recurring organizational problems tempered his pride in COPE's achievement. McDevitt ended his report to the Executive Council on the 1960 campaign with a complaint that local unions still refused to surrender their membership lists to state COPEs. Without these lists state COPEs could not check the registration status of members or break down the union membership by congressional district in order to target mailings.[1]

At COPE area conferences in 1961, McDevitt spoke of other organizational problems that COPE encountered. In Pensacola, Florida, McDevitt informed the delegates at the meeting "That the labor movement has been very successful in the economic field...but even though we had good contracts, we could not guarantee that our contracts will be fulfilled unless we kept ourselves strong in the political field." Discussions at the conference later revealed that "our COPE program breaks down at the local level." It was recommended that local union leaders appoint more shop stewards to their local union COPE committee to provide members with information on COPE endorsements and issues.

McDevitt then repeated his charge that the affiliated unions were guilty of neglecting COPE. Every president of an affiliated union was informed of the meeting in Pensacola and was requested to have staff present. Only 17 union representatives appeared. McDevitt pointed to the disappointing turnout of staff representatives as proof for his charge that the affiliated unions failed to take their political responsibilities seriously. According to one staff member at the meeting, "He [McDevitt] is firmly convinced that the reason why we are not getting our program to the membership is that the leadership of the unions are not convinced that political action is needed."[2]

At the 52nd convention of the Building and Construction Trades in 1961, McDevitt spoke frankly of the lack of cooperation COPE received from the affiliated unions.

> I tell you without fear of contradiction, we don't have a problem with the rank and file once we get to them. Our problem is with the leadership. You have one officer who puts his foot in the door and we can't get a chance to tell the story to the membership....Give us the leadership and your problems of repressive legislation are over.[3]

Later in the year, McDevitt made a similar plea before the Plumbers Union. At their national convention he promised an end to punitive labor legislation if the unions extended COPE greater cooperation and support. "If we gain forty seats in the House there'll be no more Taft-Hartley and no more Landrum-Griffin."[4]

COPE's inability to reach the membership was also a subject for discussion at the Conference on State and Local Bodies hosted by the AFL-CIO in Washington, D.C. in 1962. Prior to the conference, COPE Deputy Director Al Barkan asked each COPE area director in the field to submit a list of problems that COPE programs encountered in their jurisdiction. While some of the items submitted by Dan Powell, COPE area director for the Deep South, were limited to his district, many were general problems that could be found elsewhere.

Powell reported that "Financing COPE campaign activities or even routine COPE programs is a major problem."[5] State and local COPEs lacked the money to execute programs expected of them: check if members are registered, inform them of COPE endorsements, and financially support endorsed candidates. Though a general problem that arose elsewhere, the financial strain on COPE programs in Powell's jurisdiction was particularly acute. The amount of money that state and local central bodies in Powell's district could raise for COPE programs was limited by the small percentage of the workforce that was unionized in Alabama, Mississippi, Louisiana, Tennessee, and Arkansas. In addition, affiliation rates to state central bodies were lower in the South than they were elsewhere. Thus, state central bodies in the South found it exceedingly difficult to fund and staff statewide COPE programs.

A second problem in his jurisdiction, Powell informed Barkan, was a lack of unity and mutual respect among local unions. This manifested itself in two ways. First, a lack of unity among local unions made it difficult to get the necessary two-thirds majority required at state COPE conventions to endorse a candidate. Powell complained that

"Prior to the COPE convention, candidates have made individual deals with various international union representatives, business agents, and local union presidents and officers making it extremely difficult to get the necessary majority for one candidate at the COPE convention."[6] Powell reported that it was not unusual for a candidate to colonize a local union by promising to represent its market interests while in office. These locals then became vigorous defenders of their legislative spokesperson, no matter how noxious his or her voting record on matters of concern to the wider labor movement. For instance, public officials who supported state Davis-Bacon laws were guaranteed the support of the building trades regardless of their voting record on other issues pertinent to organized labor in the state. Thus, at state COPE conventions, the building trades would prevent candidates who opposed officials that supported Davis-Bacon from receiving the convention's endorsement. Powell noted that local unions took advantage of the two-thirds rule needed for endorsement to stalemate conventions and protect candidates who supported their market objectives.

In addition to problems caused by local unions that took advantage of endorsement rules, Powell also noted that local unions did not always respect COPE endorsements once they were issued. Powell complained "labor leaders in some cities and counties will endorse candidates in opposition to the COPE endorsed candidate."[7] These political renegades discouraged those who worked in COPE campaigns and undermined the political influence of unions in the area.

A third aspect of COPE's program that Powell suggested should be reviewed at the conference was political education. He maintained that right-wing organizations did a better job than COPE of reaching union members with their analysis of issues and candidates. COPE distributed literature to the central labor councils that informed members of the danger to their living standards posed by right-wing organizations. But this material was not reaching the rank and file. Powell wrote Barkan, "While the Group Research Reports exposing the leaders of these right-wing organizations could be an effective counter-weapon, these reports are not being used by the state and city central officer."[8]

COPE's failure to meet the challenge of right-wing organizations, however, was symptomatic of a deeper problem, an inability to communicate with the rank and file. Powell called this "the greatest problem we face in COPE campaigns."[9] Gaining access to the membership to even begin to describe to it the dangers that right-wing organizations posed to the labor movement was challenging in itself. Powell wrote:

> Probably less than 5 percent of the membership regularly attend meetings. A high percentage of plant gate leaflets are unread....City ordinances restrict the use of sound trucks at plant gates and in neighborhoods in many of the

cities and counties.

House to house front door distribution is costly, or requires a large number of volunteer workers often very difficult to secure. To reach the membership by advertising on radio, television or in daily newspapers is prohibitively costly.[10]

Powell attempted to address the problems that he enumerated in his letter to Barkan. He developed a plan of action for state councils in his district patterned after a program developed by the Louisiana state AFL-CIO. The circumstances that made the Louisiana state council an innovator are instructive. In 1954 the Louisiana state legislature passed a right-to-work law. In response, the merged Louisiana AFL-CIO held a special convention prior to the 1956 elections to defeat those responsible for the bill and have it repealed. Local unions at the convention agreed to pay a special $1.00 per capita tax to a separate fund for statewide political activity over and above their normal dues to the state federation. Eleven offices were set up throughout the state and equipped with typewriters, card files, and staff to check voting registrations. The experiment was a success. The display of union political muscle in the 1956 elections persuaded the Louisiana state legislature to restrict right-to-work in its application. The results achieved by the state council also attracted new support for it. Local unions that were skeptical of the high dues they were asked to pay were now convinced of the wisdom of this policy and voted to make the dues increase permanent. Powell wrote the national COPE office, "Had the State Council not been successful in getting the 'Right-to-Work' repealed it is doubtful they could have gotten the local unions to agree to such a per capita tax."[11]

Powell formalized and tried to sell the Louisiana example to other states in his jurisdiction under the title of Program of Progress. Program of Progress called for state labor organizations to establish a set of legislative proposals to be pursued over a period of time, to develop a public relations campaign in support of these proposals, and to create a separate financial account that was to fund this campaign. Special charges for political activity that were as high as $1.00 (Alabama) or $1.50 (Arkansas)—in some cases doubling the per capita dues that local unions owed their state federation—were assessed. Eventually, every state in the South (with the exception of Georgia) adopted a Program of Progress.

The circumstances that led to the development of Programs of Progress in the South confirm the seriousness of the financial problems that Powell touched on in his letter to Barkan. Every state labor organization in Powell's jurisdiction operated at a deficit and was thus unable to support a credible statewide COPE program. For instance, in 1960 the Mississippi AFL-CIO was running a monthly deficit of $900 at the time the Program of Progress was adopted.[12] The South Carolina state council was so hard pressed that it could not even afford to support full-time officers. The president of the council was a full-time business agent for an IBEW local and the secretary-treasurer a full-time business agent for the Textile Workers Union. Powell hoped that the creation of these special programs would ease the financial burden on state organizations. With the establishment of a Program of Progress, the costs of the statewide COPE program would be transferred to the separate account for political activity and thus no longer drain general funds. In a letter to McDevitt, Powell reviewed the financial plight of the Arkansas AFL-CIO and how approval of a Program of Progress might relieve its financial distress.

> The state AFL-CIO is absolutely unable at this time to pay the full costs of Ellison's [Arkansas COPE Director] salary and expenses. For the past year, the Council has been operating at a deficit of $700 and $800 a month, which has almost exhausted the treasury. In order to balance the budget, all routine COPE personnel and operating expenses will be transferred to the Program of Progress when the Program is adopted.[13]

Leaders of state organizations in the South worked with Powell to produce a Program of Progress for their state. The dues called for in Powell's design were so high that the program needed to be sold at each level of the labor hierarchy within a state, from district directors of affiliated unions to approval at local union meetings and then finally at statewide labor conventions. Regardless of the audience the pitch was always the same: Programs of Progress were the only protection local unions had against restrictive labor laws at the state level.

Some local unions balked at the high dues required by the program. At a special convention of the Mississippi state AFL-CIO to consider passage of a Program of Progress, an attempt to reduce the special assessment for political work from $1.50 to $1.00 was defeated by a vote of 71-10. Subsequently, the district director of the Amalgamated Clothing Workers, the second largest union in the state, disaffiliated his locals, claiming they could not afford the additional dues required by the new program.[14]

But many secondary labor leaders found the rationale for passage of a Program of Progress compelling. Louisiana created the model on which Programs of Progress were based only after passage of a right-to-work law. Similarly, local unions in Mississippi adopted a Program of Progress after organized labor failed to prevent a right-to-work provision from being added to the Mississippi state constitution by referendum. Such threats to union security attracted new locals to affiliate despite the program's high per capita charges. Following passage of the program in Arkansas, George Ellison wrote McDevitt, "Locals who disaffiliated in the past want to discuss reaffiliation."[15] In Mississippi the state council of Carpenters encouraged all of its locals to affiliate with the state organization once the program was adopted. In Arkansas and North Carolina passage of a Program of Progress also attracted new affiliations from local unions.

Passage of a Program of Progress created new possibilities for state organizations. Following approval of the program in Mississippi, state COPE Director Thomas Knight informed National COPE Director Al Barkan in Washington, D.C., "For the first time in the history of the labor movement in Mississippi it is now possible to communicate with every affiliated member by mail."[16] Address plates were cut for each member which meant that mailings could now be organized according to county, central labor body, or congressional district within the state. In addition, state labor organizations were now in a better position to assist their local central bodies. The state organization could subsidize the rental of office space and the purchase of equipment so that local central councils could engage in political work more actively and effectively.

But as much as Programs of Progress attempted to strengthen COPE structures, in the end, little progress was made. First, the establishment of such programs did not go beyond the South. Other state organizations were not in quite such financial straits as those in the South. Nor were they as beset by restrictive state and local laws which made affiliated locals amenable to the substantial costs the program entailed. But even where such programs were implemented, their impact was not as great as was hoped. Despite repeated requests from state organizations, local unions failed to divulge their membership lists so that a statewide mailing list could be compiled. In addition, local central bodies continued to form as capable leaders were found and then to dissolve as they grew weary. The state organization could invigorate local central bodies, but not resuscitate them.

But, ultimately, in the South, Programs of Progress were overwhelmed by events, especially the race issue. Local unions in the South disaffiliated from their state organizations over the race issue faster than Programs of Progress could attract new locals to replace them. Thus any financial or organizational benefits state organizations might have enjoyed as a result of passage of these programs were nullified. Even Powell who was never shy in promoting the program he developed conceded, "Alabama was the first state to adopt the Program of Progress (1960), but racial hatred stirred by George Wallace and the Klan have badly divided the ranks of labor and greatly restricted political and legislative progress under the program."[17] Programs of Progress provided state organizations with ballast but were not strong enough to serve as rudders in the midst of turmoil over civil rights for blacks. The best gauge of the effectiveness of Programs of Progress is the legislative record. On this score, the long-term legislative goals listed in Programs of Progress were as likely to be met through federal action as action taken at the state level, if satisfied at all.[18]

THE SOUTHERN STRATEGY

COPE increased its partisan activity on behalf of the Democratic party following the 1960 elections. Philip Weightman and his staff from the minorities division of COPE, Earl Davis and Fannie Neal, worked in the New Jersey gubernatorial election of 1961 to increase minority registration. They were joined by three staff members from the National Democratic Committee (NDC) and one from the New Jersey Democratic State Committee. This team worked through the framework of the New Jersey Democratic party to organize registration campaigns among blacks in Middlesex, Atlantic, Essex, Camden, Hudson, Mercer, and Passaic counties.[19]

In the 1962 elections COPE continued to employ its Northern strategy to defeat the conservative coalition in Congress. The 1962 registration drive under the direction of Victor Reuther was again targeted for urban areas of the Northeast and Midwest where union members and blacks were concentrated. In Cleveland local Auto Workers Union officials contacted black ministers, professionals, and businessmen to enlist their cooperation in a campaign to register blacks throughout the city.[20] In Harlem COPE furnished CORE with leaflets and other material to assist that organization's efforts to register voters. The national registration campaign was budgeted at $750,000 and was again to be financed by a charge on affiliated unions separate from the quota they were supposed to submit to COPE. COPE also paid for polls on behalf of Democratic candidates, another form of assistance it offered the Party beginning with 1962.[21] Ties to the Democratic party continued to grow stronger. In 1963 members of the NDC and COPE worked together to develop voting profiles for selected cities and states. The potential for increasing the black vote in targeted areas was researched.[22] Members of the NDC also now traveled with the COPE caravan to area conferences where COPE officials met with union staff representatives, local union presidents, and state and local labor officials.

COPE, however, now combined its registration activity in the North with an effort in the South to defeat the other half of the conservative coalition: Southern Democrats. But the only chance for labor to change the complexion of Southern politics was to enfranchise blacks. With so few union members in the South and a large group of unregistered blacks, the arithmetic in favor of a black-labor coalition was compelling. In 1961 Earl Davis wrote McDevitt, "In addition to members of organized labor, those outside of the labor movement will have to be made qualified to vote. We will have to bolster our Negro-labor alliance if any liberal candidate is to have a chance of reelection."[23] A first tentative step towards forging such a coalition was taken in 1957 when COPE provided money and in-kind assistance to a black voter registration group called the Alabama State Coordinating Association for Registration and Voting (ASCARV) under the direction of W.C. Patton of the NAACP.[24] Later, Fannie Neal would be assigned to work for ASCARV, to organize registration campaigns and conduct clinics throughout Alabama, though her salary and expenses would be paid by COPE.[25]

Meanwhile, Earl Davis worked closely with the Montgomery Improvement Association (MIA), which had coordinated the Montgomery bus boycott in 1956. Davis conducted workshops on voter registration for MIA, held clinics to teach people to fill out their voter registration forms accurately, and helped to organize churches and ministers in Montgomery to participate in a voter registration drive.[26] At a mass meeting of the MIA, Davis passed out sample ballots and urged those present to vote the entire COPE ticket, a request that MIA President Dr. Martin Luther King seconded.[27] Davis reported to McDevitt that he had met with the Executive Board of MIA and that they had expressed a real interest in voter registration, and that when help was needed "Dr. King came through on every request we made of him."[28]

But any effort on the part of organized labor to intervene in Southern racial matters would receive a hostile reception from members there. The response of white union members to school desegregation efforts presaged trouble.

In Tennessee, local unions mobilized quickly to oppose a resolution the Chattanooga labor council had passed. This resolution supported the local school board's decision to comply with the Supreme Court's *Brown v. Board of Education* decision. At the council's next meeting, opposition to its declared policy was so intense and widespread that the council was forced to retreat explaining, "Because of the highly controversial nature of the issues raised by the Supreme Court's decision on segregation in the public schools, issues which cut across our ranks, tending to divide us, it is hereby declared to be the policy of the Chattanooga Central Labor Union henceforth to refrain from involving itself in either side of the isssue...."[29]

In Arkansas Powell reported strong antiblack feelings among local union leaders following the Little Rock school incident. "A year ago there appeared to be less racial tension in Little Rock than in any other city in my territory, but today the racial tensions are higher here than even in Birmingham, Alabama."[30] He told McDevitt that racial tension had so "paralyzed the state and local labor leadership" that Little Rock COPE had failed to endorse or recommend any candidates for director of the new city-manager government.[31] On the heels of the turmoil at Little Rock Central High School, Bill Williams, Executive Secretary of the Arkansas AFL-CIO, wrote Ben Segal of the Southern Regional Council, "[Members] who long ago accepted the Negro in their unions, have now joined with the White America and White Citizens Council to fight school integration....The present situation is so charged with emotion that I believe we all agree that it is very difficult to go about solving the problem intelligently right now."[32]

In Alabama several local unions wrote to AFL-CIO President

Meany to protest the AFL-CIO's policy on integration and threatened to withdraw from the AFL-CIO.[33]   At the Hayes Aircraft Plant in Birmingham, Alabama, 3,200 autoworkers reportedly formed a dual union, Southern Aircraft Workers, to decertify the UAW. Later, members from the Auto Workers, Steelworkers, Communication Workers, and other unions met in Birmingham to form a rival trade union federation, Southern Crafts Inc., that would defend segregation.[34]   But, again, school integration crystalized the differences separating the labor leadership and the rank and file.   Both George Meany and Walter Reuther made public statements in support of Autherine J. Lucy's attempt to break the color line at the University of Alabama.   The *New York Times* reported that the admission of Ms. Lucy to the university "has set organized labor back twenty years in this area."   A labor leader explained that attendance at a scheduled COPE dinner was low because union members wondered, "why should they contribute money that is going to be used against them to fight segregation....These men believe in segregation and they believe that the Northern liberals who have never been in the South have no right to intervene."[35]

Organized labor could provide no greater assistance to black civil rights organizations than to provide them with sorely needed funds. But no act by unions would so inflame the membership as this. Just prior to the special convention in Mississippi that would consider passage of the Program of Progress, newspapers reported that the Industrial Unions Department of the AFL-CIO had contributed $5,000 to CORE to help defray expenses incurred by the freedom rides. Protests poured into the offices of the Mississippi state council.   Mississippi state AFL-CIO President Claude Ramsay feared the disclosure would jeopardize passage of the program at the special convention.[36] J. M. Franklin, a member of Communication Workers Local 3519 in Gulfport, Mississippi, asked Ramsay why he "and other state heads of labor have not voiced opposition to union money being sent to Mississippi to aid the freedom riders who have broken our laws."[37] Ramsay wrote Meany to explain that he was prepared to take into account the needs of the AFL-CIO, but the AFL-CIO in Washington had to appreciate the pressures under which he worked in Mississippi.   He told Meany that he understood "the AFL-CIO can take only one position, and that is against racial discrimination....Unfortunately, a wide segment of our membership doesn't know these things or don't give a damn, for today a lot of turmoil exists because of this contribution....The thing boils down to this, we can overcome everything but the contribution of union funds.   No explanation will satisfy these people in this respect."[38] In protest over the IUD's contribution, Communication Workers Local 3902 in Alabama wrote to Meany and to their international president to demand a refund for that part of their membership dues which went to the IUD.[39] In Alexandria, Louisiana, local unions issued a statement to assure the public that they were opposed to the Freedom Riders and "that as far as we can determine no union money from the state of Louisiana was contributed to these lawbreakers."[40]

Yet money was what civil rights groups needed most and COPE's Southern strategy depended on its ability to supply them with it. Arrangements for COPE to funnel money discreetly to civil rights groups were planned. As a multiracial and multipurpose organization, the Southern Regional Council (SRC) was chosen as a conduit to funnel AFL-CIO money to black voter registration groups. Wiley Branton, director of the Voter Education Project (VEP), a program run under the auspices of SRC, met with Barkan, McDevitt, Philip Weightman, and Victor Reuther in the summer of 1962. They agreed that the two groups shared common goals, should keep each other informed of current and planned activities, and exchange views regarding local groups and personalities in the South. At the meeting, COPE officials indicated they could not spend much money in the South but would provide financial assistance as requested by VEP.

The first voter registration group to which COPE was asked to contribute was the Coordinating Council of Greater New Orleans (CCGNO), a membership organization of 125 social, fraternal, and religious groups. COPE agreed to contribute $5,000, and in the summer of 1962 the first check from COPE for $1,500 was sent. But the registration effort in New Orleans stalled when the director of the project took a job outside the area. CCGNO reorganized and submitted a new project description to VEP for approval. The new project was budgeted at $25,000 with VEP to raise $15,000 of that total from outside sources. Earl Davis assured Branton that the remaining $3,500 which COPE still owed CCGNO from its initial commitment of $5,000 could be used toward the money that VEP pledged it would raise. In the fall another check from COPE for $1,750 was sent to CCGNO. On February 5, 1963, Branton flew to Washington, D.C. to meet with COPE officials to discuss the New Orleans project. Branton argued that since VEP was bearing costs in the South for voter registration that COPE would otherwise have had to carry, COPE should "seriously consider any request for financial assistance to a project from VEP." McDevitt assured Branton that COPE intended to pay the remaining $1,750 it owed on its $5,000 commitment. He then asked Branton how much additional money VEP was requesting of COPE. Branton wanted COPE to pick up all of it, the remaining $12,000 VEP said it would raise for CCGNO. McDevitt demurred. Branton reminded McDevitt that in Memphis VEP declined to give money to a group that favored a candidate COPE had opposed. Branton then warned that if VEP could not expect support from COPE then "there was no necessity for VEP to keep COPE informed of our activities or even welcome suggestions from them as to where VEP might work."[41] McDevitt reluctantly agreed to contribute an additional $6,500 to CCGNO on top of its original contribution of $5,000. By 1964, when the civil rights movement was in full stride, COPE would be giving CCGNO $1,000 a month.

But COPE's financial support of CCGNO and other voter

registration groups in the South had to be done covertly, without publicity, for fear of the reaction from members if COPE's contributions were exposed. Labor officials were so concerned that their contributions would be disclosed that they denied supporting civil rights groups when inquiries were made. In 1962 Elliot Gage, the president of an Oil, Chemical and Atomic Workers local in Memphis, wrote to AFL-CIO Secretary-Treasurer William Schnitzler to verify whether a report by newspaper columnist, Victor Riesel, was true. Riesel alleged that COPE was planning to conduct a registration drive in concert with Dr. Martin Luther King. Schnitzler referred the letter to McDevitt to respond. McDevitt replied to Gage, "I emphatically deny that we will give any part of our registration money to these minority groups or any other minority group. I assure you that we are not associated with these groups. Our drive in the AFL-CIO is conducted by us among our own members."[42] In response to a similar letter from a union member in Louisiana who inquired whether COPE had contributed money to the NAACP, Powell prevaricated. He responded that "National COPE does not make contributions to any associations or organizations outside of the AFL-CIO."[43] But this was patently untrue as COPE was actively engaged in channeling money to VEP and to local voter registration groups like ASCARV and CCGNO.

Disclaimers, even when false, could not dispel the impression that COPE and civil rights groups were allied. Support for COPE was hard to generate under such circumstances. George Ellison, Arkansas state COPE director, wrote to McDevitt, "Some of the officers of this [state] council are a little hesitant to start the COPE dollar drive because of the propaganda that has been spread by local politicians that COPE is one of the largest contributors to the NAACP."[44] One local union in North Carolina was so upset at what they perceived to be the close linkages between COPE and civil rights organizations that it went so far as to write into their bylaws that "No member shall at any time take, or spend any money from or out of the Local Union No. #183 treasury for anything pertaining to COPE."[45] Despite such reactions COPE continued to finance black voter registration organizations in the South in an effort to unseat conservative Southern Democrats. Following passage of the Voting Rights Act in 1965 the AFL-CIO called a special meeting of all state council presidents from the South to discuss the best way of taking advantage of the new law. As a result of this meeting $50,000 was appropriated to support black voter registration in five Southern states.

State AFL-CIO presidents in the South were in an even more precarious position than COPE officials in Washington if news leaked that their organizations supported civil rights for blacks. Such disclosures could cost state labor leaders their jobs and jeopardize programs sponsored by the state AFL-CIO. Local unions would disaffiliate, leaving the state organization without the resources to conduct programs and activities.

Yet, even more than COPE in Washington, the leaders of state labor organizations in the South were anxious to ally with blacks. George Ellison wrote to Weightman, "I feel very strongly about registering Negro voters in the state of Arkansas. I think it is the only way labor can ever achieve its political program in this state."[46] State council leaders in the South were eager to ally with blacks for the following reasons. First, blacks in the South were located in rural counties where organized labor had few members. These counties were the home of not a few antilabor state legislators who were immune to the influence of a labor vote. If these legislators were to be removed black voters would have to do it. Ramsay explained why a black-labor coalition in his state was necessary:

> Twenty-six counties in Mississippi have a Negro popular majority. Many of labor's worst enemies in the Mississippi state legislature live in these counties: if these people are to be removed from office it will have to be with the Negro vote. To a large degree our legislative program is dependent on our ability to form alliances with these people and this we are trying to do.[47]

A second reason why Southern state labor leaders looked favorably upon a black-labor coalition was that the ability of unions to organize in rural counties was hindered by their lack of political influence in such areas. These were, however, the very regions of the South that were experiencing job growth. For instance, in Mississippi between 1951 and 1964, twice as many industrial jobs were created in rural counties north of the city of Jackson than south of it in the more economically developed regions of the state.[48] But organizers encountered great resistance from local officials and police when they tried to organize in rural counties because labor had no political influence in these areas. State labor leaders hoped that black voters would act as a counterweight to entrenched power structures in rural areas and make organizing in such regions easier.

Third, blacks and organized labor in the South faced common enemies and shared common problems. Laws intended to restrict marches and demonstrations for civil rights could be and were used to restrict picketing. Moreover, unions as well as blacks were frequently the target of White Citizens Councils, the Ku Klux Klan, and more established defenders of the "Southern way of life". Thus, it was logical that Southern union leaders should attempt to enfranchise blacks in order to strengthen the ranks against their common enemies.[49]

But as rational as it appeared for state labor leaders to ally with civil rights organizations, the risks of such a coalition were as great as the rewards. The Georgia state AFL-CIO never supported civil rights organizations to the degree state labor organizations in Mississippi, Alabama, or Arkansas did, even though the benefits of coalition were as apparent to labor leaders in Georgia as they were to leaders in other states. Though confronted with the same choices not every state labor leader in the South made the same decision. To focus on strategic reasons—such as those mentioned by Ramsay to explain why state federation leaders allied with civil rights groups—tends to minimize the heroism of their decision to do so. It does not balance the rewards of such a strategy with the very real risks it entailed. And the risks state labor leaders ran were apparent the more the civil rights struggle escalated.

The atmosphere was so charged that labor leaders who publicly opposed segregation had their lives threatened.[50] Ramsay went armed at all times and members of his family were trained to use a gun.[51] He was vilified in the newspapers, denounced in the Mississippi state legislature, and his leadership was openly repudiated by local union leaders within the state. The personal costs were so high for Ramsay and his family that, at times, he considered resigning. Only the promise of continued support by the AFL-CIO in Washington, D.C. kept him at his job.[52]

What was especially discouraging for state labor leaders was the affiliation problem. Local unions disaffiliated over the procivil rights policies followed by their state organizations. In Alabama membership in the state council declined from 93,800 in 1960 to 55,546 in 1965; just 30 percent of the AFL-CIO membership in the state.[53] Between 1962 and 1964, 34 local unions from the Steelworkers alone withdrew from the state council.[54] Alabama state President Barney Weeks wrote Powell:

> The reason for sending you all of this is to show you some small evidence of the total concentration on the race issue by so many of our members, which is costing us the loss of thousands of members in affiliations....I don't know what you can do about this, but wanted you to know something about the present situation, which is steadily deteriorating.[55]

This wave of disaffiliations forced the state council to lay off one full-time employee and close to its Montgomery office due to lack of funds.[56] At the hight of the conflict over civil rights Fannie Neal reported to COPE in Washington:

> I talked with Barney Weeks and asked what, if anything, the state organization was doing now that the Voters bill was passed. He said that due to the loss of so many members because of the Civil Rights issue, the state organization was unable to do anything financially at this time.[57]

The Arkansas state labor council also suffered a wave of disaffiliations for its support of the AFL-CIO position on civil rights. Locals first began to disaffiliate in 1957 when the state AFL-CIO convention adopted a resolution that criticized Governor Faubus's demagogic use of the Little Rock high school incident. More locals left when the president of the state council stated publicly that organized labor must do all it can to preserve free public education in Arkansas. Following the 1961 state AFL-CIO convention at which the integrationist line of the council was preserved, the state organization lost 4,000 members including almost every IBEW local within the state.[58]

But no state organization was so disrupted by the affiliation problem as the Mississippi state AFL-CIO. Powell reported to COPE in Washington that "The Radical Right-Wing's use of the racial issue to get local unions to withdraw has hurt the Mississippi Council more than it has anywhere in the South."[59] The 1964 Officer's Report to the 1964 Mississippi state AFL-CIO convention conceded, "The labor council's number one problem is that of affiliation."[60] The more Mississippi state AFL-CIO President Claude Ramsay publicly opposed segregation the more the membership melted away. Only 25 percent of all AFL-CIO members in Mississippi were affiliated with the state organization. Local 602 of the Paperworkers and Papermakers Union expressed what many locals felt when it informed the state AFL-CIO of its decision to disaffiliate, "We do not feel the State Labor Council Stands for the Same Principle and Ideals As We Do."[61] Most locals did not even give a reason for their action. They just ceased to forward their dues to the Mississippi state AFL-CIO office. Ramsay apprised Stanton Smith, AFL-CIO Coordinator of State and Local Central Bodies, of the situation, "Apparently the White Citizen Council has initiated a concerted drive to disaffiliate as many locals as possible....If you have any ideas about coping with this I'd be glad to hear from you."[62] Smith sent a letter to affiliated union presidents with local unions in Mississippi to explain the problem faced by Ramsay "who has supported AFL-CIO policy to [his] own disadvantage." Smith asked the affiliated union presidents to instruct their local unions in Mississippi to join the state organization.[63] Few complied. One union president who received a letter from Smith sympathized with Ramsay's predicament and wrote him that "since the civil rights movement they [members] have seceded from any AFL-CIO organization. We have had a hard time keeping them in our locals."[64] The financial squeeze disaffiliation created was so great that at one point Ramsay could not cash his paycheck because there was not enough money in the state AFL-CIO treasury to cover it.[65] Affiliations were so low that despite a matching grant from COPE and a subsidy of $5,000 from the AFL-CIO the Mississippi state council operated at a deficit of $700 per month in 1965.[66]

Disaffiliations crippled COPE programs in the South and jeopardized COPE's Southern strategy of defeating conservative Southern Democrats. The race issue was so powerful that state organizations responsible for overseeing statewide COPE programs could not hold their members. Even with substantial assistance from the AFL-CIO in Washington, state councils had difficulty sustaining themselves.

No incident so reveals the pressures under which state labor leaders worked than one that occurred in Mississippi. Following passage of the Voting Rights Act in 1965, the Mississippi state AFL-CIO poured its energy into registering black voters. Ramsay wrote Barkan, now COPE Director, "according to the best information available, five counties have reached or passed the fifty percent mark [for registration]. These are the counties where we have spent money up to this point." He reported that, "In Adams County, the NAACP had 16 workers canvassing house-to-house but ran out of money. I made $400 available and as a result they passed the fifty percent mark." When the NAACP carried its registration drive into an adjacent county where a federal registrar was present Ramsay contributed another $300. Ramsay informed Barkan that he hoped to assist the NAACP in organizing voter registration drives in all 14 counties of Mississippi to which federal registrars were assigned.[67]

In March 1966, the Mississippi state AFL-CIO Executive Board agreed that more formal arrangements for the labor council to work with civil rights groups were needed if labor was to take full advantage of the Voting Rights Act.[68] Vernon Jordan, director of VEP, Aaron Henry and Charles Evers from the NAACP, and Tom Knight and Claude Ramsay from the Mississippi state AFL-CIO, met to consider forming a statewide organization to register blacks to vote. The registration effort was to be concentrated in counties with large black majorities in the northwest portion of the state and was budgeted at $107,000.[69] A letter was prepared in the offices of the Mississippi labor council under the signature of Aaron Henry, president of the Mississippi NAACP, and sent to civil rights groups throughout the state. The letter invited interested parties to attend a meeting to discuss forming an organization that would run a statewide voter registration campaign. Henry indicated in his letter that "We expect to finance this campaign with Foundation and Union Funds."[70] A follow-up letter, this time signed by Ramsay, was sent four days later because the original letter accidentally omitted the time of the meeting scheduled for Jackson on April 20th. The meeting in Jackson was a success. Every relevant organization in the state, including the Mississippi Freedom Democratic Party and the NAACP which had been feuding, had at least one representative present. Flush with hope, Ramsay wrote Weightman, "I understand that this was the first time some of these people had ever attended a meeting of this kind."[71] On May 20, the Delta Democrat-Times broke the story of Ramsay's intimate involvement with the formation of the Mississippi Voter Registration and Education League (MVREL).[72] Soon the story was covered in newspapers throughout Mississippi. The response was sharp and prolonged. Local unions in Meridian, Mississippi, issued a joint statement repudiating Ramsay's actions and leadership.[73] Another union reassured the public that "it lends no support either financial or otherwise to this newly formed voter registration group in which Mr. Ramsay is active."[74] Newspaper editorials were piercing in their criticism of Ramsay's initiative.[75] Ramsay wrote to Stanton Smith, "I understand the Klan has really given me hell in their last four rallies. Instead of one shot gun loaded I am now keeping two."[76] In a statewide mailing to the membership Ramsay defended his participation in the formation of MVREL. He argued that labor needed to ally with black voters in order to thwart the efforts of the business community to do the same.[77] In one letter to a critic he challenged his respondent to confront the facts of life as they existed in Mississippi. "Many of organized labor's worst enemies live in those counties that are predominantly Negro in population. If we are to do anything about this situation we must be in a position to influence the Negro vote in those counties....If you or other members of your organization have any constructive ideas in dealing with this problem I will certainly be glad to listen to them."[78]

Ramsay's attempt to frame the issue for members as a labor-management dispute did not mute protests to his actions. Nor did it prevent Ramsay from going forward with plans to form a statewide organization to register blacks to vote. Executive Committee meetings of the MVREL were held at the offices of the Mississippi state AFL-CIO, the labor council did mailings for the MVREL, and had printed MVREL membership cards. Ramsay was chastened enough by the outcry to not serve as an officer of MVREL, but only as an unofficial advisor. But most important, the state labor organization continued to contribute money. Ramsay's files contain copies of letters to voter registration organizations throughout Mississippi in which checks from the Mississippi state AFL-CIO were enclosed.[79] He received a note from the Coahoma County Branch of the NAACP thanking him "for the finances made available to us by you that aided us in carrying out our voter registration campaign."[80] Ramsay was so identified with the voter registration effort and with MVREL that groups appealed directly to Ramsay for funds or asked him to intervene on their behalf to obtain money from MVREL.[81]

The Mississippi state council was not the only state labor organization actively involved in black voter registration efforts. Louisiana state AFL-CIO President Victor Bussie informed Emory Via at the Southern Regional Council that "We have sponsored efforts jointly with the Negro community throughout Louisiana to step up the registration program."[82] In 1964 the Arkansas state council worked with the NAACP and other black groups in support of a referendum proposal that would abolish the poll tax. Labor furnished virtually all the money and staff for this successful effort.[83] A year later Powell reported to COPE in Washington that the Arkansas state AFL-CIO was "working with Liberal and Negro leaders in the formation of a Liberal-Negro coalition for the 1966 elections."[84] In Alabama Barney Weeks withstood tremendous pressure from members in his state to give support to black voter registration efforts and to integration. In North Carolina, the Charlotte central labor council supported black voter registration groups in its vicinity.[85]

The active role state federation presidents like Ramsay played in the civil rights movement seems to contradict our earlier analysis of the organizational constraints under which such leaders act. It was argued previously that the dependence of state and local leaders on local unions prevents them from pursuing political goals, like civil rights, that are removed from the market concerns of the affiliated locals. But the contradiction is only apparent. State federations in the South were only able to pursue such political goals as civil rights for blacks because the AFL-CIO provided them with an alternative base of support. The AFL-CIO subsidized state labor organizations, mobilized its bureaucracy to assist state presidents who opposed segregation, and in Ramsay's case, guaranteed him a staff position with the AFL-CIO should his views ever cost him his job. Ramsay acknowledged that he would not have done what he did if the AFL-CIO had not stood behind him.[86] Thus, state federation presidents were able to escape the political limits imposed by their dependance on affiliated local unions because they were able to draw on the AFL-CIO as an alternative base of support.

Another reason why state labor leaders could range so far from the market concerns of local unions was due to a mistaken strategy used by their opponents. Supporters of massive resistance to integration instructed their union followers to disaffiliate as a protest against the policies of their state labor federation. This certainly weakened state federations but, due to the support of the AFL-CIO in Washington, D.C., did not leave them totally without resources to support black voter registration activity. More important, disaffiliation prevented those local unions that disagreed with their state federation's policies from mounting a challenge to them. By 1964 almost all of those locals who disagreed with the policies of their state organization had left. As a result, state labor leaders had latitude to pursue their civil rights policies because the only locals left were those who agreed with their views or were willing to live with them in order to maintain a statewide labor presence. The freedom that state federation presidents had to pursue policies beyond the market concerns of the affiliated locals was as great as the number of local unions who had left would permit. In the South in the 1960's, that was a great deal of latitude indeed.

Finally, the support that COPE and Southern state federations gave to the civil rights movement is clear evidence for Greenstone and Harrington's "social democratic party surrogate" thesis. In conjunction with state federations, COPE tried to organize a constituency interested in social democratic reform into the Democratic party. They attempted to enfranchise Southern blacks in order to unseat conservative Southern Democratic congressmen and state legislators. But the effect of this strategy was to isolate COPE from secondary labor leaders who would not cooperate in the implementation of this strategy. They either disagreed fundamentally with the policy, feared its divisive quality would hurt them politically, or doubted its trade union relevance. Nor were COPE's attempts to frame the race issue as diversionary or to place it in the context of a labor-management dispute plausible to people who felt deeply about such matters. Regardless of how it addressed the issue, COPE, the AFL-CIO, and Southern state federation leaders could not gain the cooperation and support of local union leaders for their partisan strategy. The further down the labor hierarchy one goes, the less cooperation COPE received in its effort to aggregate blacks into the Democratic party.

FROM VICTORY TO DEFEAT

In the mid-sixties, the race issue migrated from the South to the North. New York City, Newark, Los Angeles, Detroit and Cleveland were rocked by black protests. COPE now faced the same dilemma in the North that it confronted in the South: the conflict between COPE's partisan strategy to bring blacks into the Democratic Party and its organizational dependence on secondary leaders who saw little value in such activity.

In 1964, COPE's first battle was in Oklahoma where a right-to-work amendment was scheduled to appear on the ballot in May. COPE again sought the votes of blacks to defeat this proposal, just as it had done in the right-to-work referendums of 1958. Earl Davis was sent to Oklahoma City and Fannie Neal to Tulsa to work the black precincts. Black ministers in both cities were recruited to participate in the registration effort. In Tulsa the NAACP youth group was hired to canvas neighborhoods and contact unregistered voters. Pamphlets that showed the police in Alabama using water hoses and dogs against civil rights protesters were distributed with the warning "This Happened in Right-to-Work Alabama. Don't Let it Happen Here."[87] Again the results justified COPE's efforts and expense. The amendment was defeated with black precincts voting overwhelmingly against it. The *Tulsa Tribune* reported, "What was surprising was the effectiveness of the union alliance with old age and Negro groups....[The] amendment was defeated in Tulsa County by almost exactly the margin it lost the black precincts.[88]

COPE's 1964 voter registration drive was originally scheduled to begin in August. But when the Republican party issued its platform and selected Senator Barry Goldwater to head its ticket the AFL-CIO moved the starting date of its registration drive up a month. At the time of his nomination Goldwater had a perfect antiunion voting record. He had voted against labor's recommendation on every test vote used by the AFL-CIO during his congressional career. Union leaders responded vigorously to Goldwater's candidacy. Twice as many affiliated unions met their COPE quota in 1964 than had done so in 1960. Large unions like the IUE, the Retail Clerks, and the Building Service and Employees

Union, each of whom were poor contributors previously, now met their financial obligation to COPE. Collectively, the affiliated unions met 67 percent of their COPE quota, a ten percent increase over 1960, raising a total of $1,045,000.[89] In addition, the AFL-CIO levied a $0.05 per capita tax on the affiliated unions for its Voter Registration Fund. This raised an extra $900,000 for the campaign.

The threat posed to union security by Goldwater's candidacy spurred the secondary labor leadership to participate in and support COPE's registration drive. One reporter described labor in the campaign as "frightened and aroused" as never before:

> [The affiliated unions] are supporting L.B.J. with a unanimity that pervades all 130 national unions affiliated with the AFL-CIO. Goldwater has been forsaken by such devout Republicans as Maurice Hutcheson, head of the Carpenters, James Suffridge, chief of the Retail Clerks, and Lee Minton, President of the Glass Blowers....Even the conservative craft unionists in the Plumbers, Pattern Makers, and others see this as a stark confrontation between the labor movement and right-wing extremism....A major paradox of the Goldwater counterrevolution is that the Senator is providing the labor movement with the kind of advertising it has long required for political clarity and consensus.[90]

In New York City there were 21 district COPE offices set up for registration work. Los Angeles had 27 such offices to cover the city. In Illinois, 3,500 union members were poised to bring voters to the polls on election day.[91] Only in the South, where the racial issue clouded all others, was COPE unable to mobilize trade union support for the Democratic ticket. Following the election, the *AFL-CIO News* reported, "More International Unions tied their work directly to COPE operations, a number appointed full-time COPE Directors and there was close cooperation to make sure the funds went where they were needed most."[92] States in the Northeast and Midwest, as well as California and Texas, received the lion's share of the money that COPE raised. Utah, North Dakota, and Tennessee also received special financial consideration from COPE's national office. In addition COPE set aside $40,000 for minority registration.[93]

Al Barkan, now Director of COPE following McDevitt's death in 1963, worked tirelessly throughout the summer to animate the secondary leadership. He spoke frequently at affiliated union and state council conventions to make sure that union leaders had a clear idea of what was at stake in the approaching elections. In his peroration before the Kentucky state AFL-CIO he told the assembled delegates:

> This is a life and death struggle we're in. I don't care how

good your contracts are. I don't care how good your leaders are. I don't care how fat your treasuries are. You can't lick this assault on the picket line. The only way you can win this battle is at the ballot box....Nothing, absolutely nothing, is more important than the outcome of the November 3 election to your family, your union, and your future.[94]

The election results were a breathtaking success for COPE. AFL-CIO-endorsed President Johnson defeated Barry Goldwater in a landslide, receiving 61 percent of the vote. But more important, the President's coattails were long enough to elect enough liberal congressmen to depose the conservative coalition in Congress. Two-thirds of all COPE-endorsed congressmen won. COPE's batting average was only slightly lower in competitive districts where COPE won 62 percent of these races. Thirty-three COPE-endorsed Congressmen beat incumbents while only one COPE-endorsed incumbent lost. In the Senate COPE won all but six of the 30 contests in which it endorsed a candidate.[95]

Organized labor did not have to wait long to reap the rewards of its hard work. Within 100 days of its first session, the Eighty-ninth Congress passed legislation for which the unions had been lobbying over 20 years. Aid to education, aid to Appalacia, manpower-training amendments, and a drug control bill all passed in the amount of time it usually takes Congress to organize itself and hold hearings. The Eighty-ninth Congress also put medicare legislation on the President's desk. President Johnson gave the pen he used to sign the bill to George Meany in recognition of the many years the AFL-CIO had pursued such legislation. Civil rights and voting rights bills which the AFL-CIO had supported were also passed. The only piece of legislation in which labor's hopes were disappointed was repeal of section 14(b) of the Taft-Hartley Act. A bill to repeal 14(b) was passed in the House but was the object of a successful filibuster in the Senate. The successful filibuster of 14(b) only renewed the AFL-CIO's determination to increase the liberal composition of Congress in 1966. An article in *Memo From COPE* reminded union leaders of the job that lay ahead:

One figure expressed the change in the House of Representatives from the days when the Dixiecrat-conservative coalition rode high blocking good legislation to the progressive record established in the first session of the 90th Congress.

It is 51.

That's the number of new liberals you helped elect to the House in 1964. They made the difference between victory and defeat for much crucial Great Society legislation—a good point to remember in view of the 1966 elections coming up.[96]

The atmosphere at the 1965 AFL-CIO convention in San Francisco was the opposite of what it had been when the AFL-CIO last convened in that city in 1959. In 1959 the delegates were despondent over the passage of Landrum-Griffin and feared more restrictive labor legislation was imminent. In contrast, the delegates in 1965 arrived buoyant over their recent legislative success. The President's Report to the convention stated jubilantly, "The New Deal proclaimed in 1933 has come to a belated maturity under L.B.J. in 1965." But the Report warned, "we must exert every effort to make sure that the true will of the people is expressed at the polls: that confidence does not breed apathy and open the doors to reaction."[97]

Willard Shelton, writing in the *American Federationist*, found reasons for optimism when he looked ahead to 1966. First, 20 states had already reapportioned their congressional districts in line with the Supreme Court's "one man, one vote" decision. This, it was believed, would increase the electoral influence of the cities and suburbs where the liberal Democratic constituency was located and decrease the voting strength of more conservative rural areas. Secondly, Shelton expected the new Voting Rights Act to increase minority registration tremendously, especially in the South. Blacks could be counted on to vote for congressmen who had supported Great Society legislation. Third, Shelton pointed to the 1962 elections as evidence that the presidential party could avoid normal midterm losses. Finally, Shelton noted that prior to 1964, congressional candidates tended to run ahead of the presidential ticket in their districts. This indicated, he felt, a great deal of natural strength for the Party among voters. Shelton concluded:

> For those who favor the Great Society of President Johnson the issue is clear: It is to reelect those 51 freshmen members of the House, give them the advantages of a second term, gain the benefits of their votes in the 90th Congress, as well as the 89th...[and] the additional seniority that may result in a permanent shift in the political atmosphere and voting habits of these districts.[98]

Early soundings of the membership indicated that voter apathy was the greatest obstacle COPE would have to overcome in 1966. At the Auto Workers Union convention in California, the need to increase registration and dispel apathy were given a high priority. UAW leaders warned that defeat of the liberal majority in the Eighty-ninth Congress would be read as a mandate to repeal the progressive legislation just enacted.[99] George Meany told the delegates to the Building and Construction Trades Legislative conference that their support of COPE was essential if 14(b) was to be repealed when a new Congress convened.[100] In June a special meeting of the political directors of the affiliated unions was called to discuss ways to inspire the troops and prevent a low turnout in November.[101] The 1966 registration campaign was budgeted at $950,000. The AFL-CIO and IUD each pledged $125,000 for the campaign and a per capita levy on the affiliated unions was expected to net another $700,000.

But as returns from the Democratic primaries came in, fears COPE had about apathy were replaced by fears over another issue—civil rights. In Louisiana James Morrison, a 12 term Congressman and the only member of the Louisiana delegation to vote against Taft-Hartley, lost in the primaries. Even by Louisiana standards this was a vicious campaign. Morrison charged that his opponent was a member of the Ku Klux Klan, but the opposite claim, that Morrison was too soft on the race issue, proved more damaging with voters. During the campaign Morrison was turned away from union halls where he had been welcome formerly due to his failure to defend segregation strongly enough. In Maryland, representative Carleton Sickles, who had a 100 percent COPE voting record, lost in the gubernatorial primary to George Mahoney. Mahoney had run a one-note campaign of uncompromising opposition to open housing. He outpolled Sickles in the white, working-class wards of Baltimore (wards 20-26) by a margin of 2-to-1. Mahoney was regarded as such an open racist by the Maryland-D.C. AFL-CIO that it endorsed a little-known county executive by the name of Spiro Agnew in the general election. COPE suffered another loss in the Senate primary race in Tennessee. Ross Bass, who occupied the seat formerly held by Kefauver, was defeated by Governor Frank Clement. Bass had a COPE voting record of 48 "right" votes and only 10 "wrong."

The change in outlook that occurred over the summer is recounted in a letter that Helmuth Kern, political director for the Amalgamated Meatcutters, sent to COPE staffpeople following the election:

> At the beginning of the summer it looked as if the customary midterm losses of the Party in power would particularly hurt conservative Democratic congressmen in the South, and it looked as if most of our liberal and moderate friends would return and even a majority of the newly elected liberal congressmen. They had produced one of the greatest legislative records in the history of the United States, and contributed to social progress beyond belief. However, they were confronted in their right for reelection by a vicious issue, which strangely enough was kept silent and hushed up: Integration—Civil Rights.[102]

COPE confronted the race issue obliquely rather than directly. Barkan saw the race issue as a false one cleverly thrown into the campaign by labor's opponents. It was a ploy to wean members from voting their economic interests, the defense of welfare state programs just enacted. He told a reporter, "Labor's enemies are trying to divert trade unionists from the real issues to trick them into voting against labor's proven friends."[103]

In October Barkan told delegates to the Papermakers convention that he was "uneasy" over the success union-busters had "amongst our own members" in using racial fears to deflect members from the real issues. He urged delegates to go back to their local unions and "do an educational job with our own people. We've got to show them friend from foe. We've got to show them the real issues from the phony issues."[104] Two weeks later at the Chemical Workers convention, Barkan clarified what the real issues of the campaign were. "The real issue is not racial strife, as serious as that is. For men and women of labor, what is more important to us than a job, a good steady job, a job with dignity, a job with security?"[105]

Union presidents who identified with COPE also described the race issue as a subterfuge when they spoke at union gatherings, but their tone was even more apocolyptic. Those candidates who promoted racial division did not only intend to halt social progress, but hoped to use the issue as a trojan horse for restrictive labor legislation. Joseph Keenan, president of the IBEW, spoke to the California labor COPE convention and argued that unions in California faced the same challenge in 1966 as they faced in 1958 when they had to contend with a right-to-work proposal on the state ballot. According to Keenan, the civil rights issue was simply a front under which labor's opponents planned to "grab the governor's office so that they can achieve their right-to-work program."[106] Ray Siemiller, president of the Machinists Union, warned delegates to the Alabama state council convention that "right wingers have found that they can divide the working people and obscure their antilabor programs by stirring up racial antagonism." Union members had to choose between "a militant trade union attitude" and racial demagogues who opposed unemployment insurance, workmen's compensation, and trade unions.[107] I. W. Abel, president of the Steelworkers Union, sent a letter to every member of his union alerting them to the "crisis facing your Union and the entire labor movement in next month's national election." He pleaded with them not to let their "justifiable concern over recent rioting to affect their better judgement in choosing candidates....No one in his right mind approves of riots....But we must not kid ourselves, electing labor's enemies in November will not cause these problems to disappear.[108] Memo from COPE reiterated these messages when it asked, "Who really is behind the race hate injected into the campaign? Who's using it to obscure the real issues?...It's all the groups ranged against you, and your welfare, and your union—the John Birch Society and other right extremists, the racists and the right-to-workers and their allies."[109]

Although the membership wavered over the civil rights revolution, organized labor continued to solidify its alliance with those groups that promoted it. The Louisiana state AFL-CIO invested heavily in black voter registration to ensure that congressman Hale Boggs did not meet the same fate in the general election as his colleague James Morrison met in the primaries.[110] In Tennessee, national and state COPE staff members worked with and financially supported the black leadership in Knoxville, Chattanooga and Nashville to get out the vote. In North Carolina COPE supported black voter registration groups in the eighth and sixth congressional districts, and in Arkansas the state council helped finance car pools to take black voters to the polls.[111]

But as the campaign neared its climax, COPE strategists were unsure whether they would be able to contain the centrifugal forces that separated blacks and white union members. A Gallup poll found that, for the first time since 1962, a majority felt the Administration had pushed civil rights too far.[112] Barkan told the *New York Times*, "Who can tell what this madness [white backlash] is going to do? This is our biggest problem."[113] Meany made one final plea and called for the reelection of "all the liberals in the 89th Congress" and the defeat of those "who fought progress, fought President Johnson, and fought labor....The 89th Congress did its job. Now its up to labor to do our job at the polls on election day."[114]

The 1966 election results were a devastating blow to everyone involved in labor's campaign. Hopes were shattered for building upon the welfare state record of the Eighty-ninth Congress and for repeal of 14(b). The Democrats lost 47 seats in the House, more than the Republicans had lost in the Goldwater debacle two years earlier. Thirty-six incumbents with COPE voting records of 75 percent or better were defeated. Less than half of all COPE incumbents from competitive districts retained their seats. The number of congressmen considered friendly to labor dropped from 248 to 199. In the Senate COPE lost 13 out of 22 contests where it issued an endorsement. Barkan admitted after the returns were in, "I'm flabbergasted. We took a terrible beating."[115]

COPE's attempt to move the arena of conflict away from the racial issue had failed. By not addressing the race issue directly the opposition was able to define it for the membership. Looking back on the campaign, Helmuth Kern, political director for the Amalgamated Meatcutters, wrote:

> What needed to be done during the campaign was not to scare the owners of little homes who are afraid to lose their total life savings invested in their property, but to dramatically and tirelessly convince them and prove to these voters that civil rights and civil rights legislation does [sic] not mean block busting and is not identical with destroying white neighborhoods....[116]

COPE's post-election analysis of the results found evidence of backlash among union voters, expressed often in non-voting.[117]

TABLE 5-1: RETURNS FROM WHITE, BLUE-COLLAR WARDS IN
SELECT CITIES IN 1962 AND 1966: NON-VOTING

City	Party	1962	1966
Detroit (gub)	D	52,843 (78.7%)	33,558 (69.5%)
(wards 13, 17, 19)	R	14,269 (21.3%)	14,637 (30.5%)
Cincinnati (gub)	D	11,006 (47.0%)	6,838 (34.8%)
(wards 19, 20, 21, 25)	R	12,405 (53.0%)	12,788 (65.2%)
Philadelphia (gub)	D	197,029 (60.0%)	83,597 (51.3%)
(wards 26, 31, 33, 36, 39, 43, 48)	R	131,379 (40.0%)	77,910 (48.7%)
Louisville (sen.)	D	9,071 (53.6%)	4,970 (43.2%)
(wards 5, 8)	R	8,154 (46.4%)	6,547 (56.8%)

Table 5-1 indicates that while the Republican gubernatorial candidate hardly made any gains from white, blue-collar wards in Detroit and Cincinnati, support for the Democratic candidate declined 37 percent in each city compared to 1962 totals. In Philadelphia and Louisville, Democratic support in the gubernatorial race from white, blue-collar wards dropped 58 and 46 percent respectively from 1962 totals. California was one of the few areas where backlash was expressed in vote-switching and not nonvoting.[118]

Barkan expressed his regret about how union members voted in the election in a letter to Roy Wilkins, head of the NAACP. He told Wilkins, "We in COPE are sharply aware that many of our own union members deserted liberal candidates for one reason only: In protest against their advocacy of civil rights." Barkan assured Wilkins that COPE had tried to educate union members. But as the election returns indicated "Apparently, however, we have not done enough."[119]

Part of the reason why COPE's effort to shift the terrain of conflict away from race had failed was that old problems had returned to haunt COPE. Without a threat to union security that could spontaneously mobilize and unite the unions politically—as Goldwater's candidacy had done in 1964—it was difficult to inspire local union leaders to do anything politically. Reports from local unions of the Amalgamated Meatcutters reveal some of the problems that COPE experienced in this regard. Local 66 in St. Louis admitted that it undertook no activity on behalf of COPE because "We have no full or part-time staff to spearhead an efficient program." Local unions in Maine, Hawaii, Utah, and Washington also complained to the Amalgamated's national office in Chicago that they lacked the necessary staff and money to do anything for COPE. Other locals reported that they did cooperate with COPE, but that other local unions did not. Local 33 of the Amalgamated Meatcutters in Springfield, Massachusetts reported that "Other unions did zero. Perhaps we will conduct our own area phone and voter pool in the future." Another local union complained, "Many of the International unions spoke big but did nothing." Local 350 in Gary, Indiana averred that "Labor unions would be more effective on Election Day if they were not divided. Some construction locals endorsed Halleck for Congress against McFadden, who received COPE's endorsement." Kern drew the following lesson from these local union reports which he shared in a letter to COPE's leaders:

> Our methods as well as our approach need careful analysis in order to enable us to do a better job in the future. The most important lesson of all is that the trade union movement and COPE cannot hammer together a gerrymade organization every time an election comes around, but we must have a year-round well-planned and well-programmed COPE operation, which does not have to start from scratch when it is called into operation.[120]

But the soul searching went further than this. The election indicated that COPE was not getting its message through to union members. One internal report on the election conceded, "Union political education undoubtedly has kept things from getting worse, but in elections such as that of this past November we have seen countless union men and their wives vote against their best interests. We realize that our political education work has not been adequate. We realize that we are not entirely getting through to the rank and file."[121]

George Meany was so shocked by the results that he instructed COPE to conduct a survey of the political attitudes of union members in order to discover exactly what had gone wrong in the election. COPE turned this task over to John Kraft, Inc., a professional polling firm that COPE had used previously to do polls for favored candidates. The Kraft poll was "the most thorough and complex survey among union members ever conducted." Its sample included 1,700 union members located in 47 states and belonging to 12 different affiliated unions.[122]

The public first became aware of the poll's existence when some of its controversial results were revealed in an article by James P. Gannon that appeared in the *Wall Street Journal.* Gannon reported that the "poll's political findings were shocking....Labor's traditional legislative goals are out of line with union members' main interests."[123] According to Gannon, the poll found only minimal support among union members for such items as increasing unemployment insurance, social security, the minimum wage, or for repeal of 14(b). In addition, members were said to be disenchanted with President Johnson and in disagreement with the AFL-CIO on such matters as civil rights and social welfare legislation. In Gannon's recapitulation of the poll, demographic changes were responsible for the gap between the leadership and the membership that the poll had identified. The typical union member was younger than the AFL-CIO leadership and was to be found living in the suburbs in his own home. These members were more concerned with such issues as property taxes, crime, zoning regulations, and water rates than the welfare state agenda pursued by the AFL-CIO. Moreover, this new breed of union member viewed his union instrumentally and did not identify with it in any personal way.

The Associated Press wire service picked up Gannon's article and gave it wide distribution. Barkan was stung by the impression the article gave that the AFL-CIO leadership was out of touch with its members politically. He countered and released some of the data from the poll. In fact, Gannon had never actually seen the poll, but had based his story on what his sources within the AFL-CIO told him it contained. When Barkan released some of the poll's findings—six months after the poll was conducted—it was the first time any of the data from the poll was made public.

Barkan's article on the poll was scheduled to be published in the August issue of the *American Federationist*, but galleys of what was to appear were released early to the press. Barkan's article began with the clear statement, "Union members today would vote overwhelmingly for President Johnson against any potential Republican candidate. They support the President's legislative achievements and endorse the legislative goals of the AFL-CIO and the President." Barkan then went on to correct some of the inaccuracies that appeared in Gannon's account of the Kraft poll. For example, Gannon reported, "The AFL-CIO number one goal in this session of Congress—boosting social security payments—drew more boos than cheers." Gannon had also indicated that union members supported a variety of prospective Republican presidential candidates over President Johnson in 1968. In fact, respondents were not even queried on their support for social security and they did favor President Johnson over any of the Republicans he was placed against. According to Barkan, "The Kraft poll on the whole is encouraging. It indicates that the policy positions adopted by the AFL-CIO Convention accurately reflect the feelings of the union membership, with the single exception of open occupancy housing."[124]

But Barkan's analysis was for public consumption only. Union leaders, in truth, found the results of the Kraft poll disquieting. The director of organizing for the Sheet Metal Workers wrote a lengthy and personal appraisal of the Kraft poll from which he drew the following lesson, "The fault Dear Brutus lies not in our stars but in ourselves."[125] Another individual who reached a far different and far less optimistic conclusion than Barkan was John Kraft himself, whose organization conducted the poll. At COPE area conferences in 1967 Kraft pointed to problems revealed by the poll that Barkan's account either understated or left unmentioned. According to Kraft, "The study makes it abundantly clear there are serious gaps in the identification of union members with what may be their own interests—and that the communications problem is particularly severe among younger—people under thirty—members."

Kraft's analysis drew attention to the same group of young union members that Gannon had identified earlier as most restive. Such members constituted a growing proportion of the union population—one-half of all union members were under forty years of age—and were most likely to be suburban homeowners. This group, Kraft found, was least likely to share the perspective of the AFL-CIO leadership. For instance, when asked to rate the salience of different issues, it was no surprise that the Vietnam War, civil rights, and the economy figured prominently in the answers Kraft received. But many union members, especially those under forty, also described typical suburban problems like fair tax assessment, crime, zoning laws, and street and sewer repair as significant issues.

Kraft also inquired whether the leadership and membership shared common views on issues and again Kraft was disturbed at what he found. One quarter of all union members disagreed with or had no opinion on increasing workmen's compensation; one-third opposed or took no stand on increasing the minimum wage; and 45 percent opposed or had no clear idea of where they stood on repeal of 14(b). In all three cases, the strongest opposition to these traditional union demands came from younger members in the suburbs.

Finally, while Kraft knew all of his respondants were union members, when asked whether they were members of any organization "only 64 percent seemed to attach enough significance to their membership to mention it as something they belonged to." Kraft found that younger members were less likely to recall their union membership than older members. On the basis of his survey Kraft concluded:

> The survey makes it pretty clear that union members do not readily identify with such labor union goals as better workmen's compensation, improved unemployment compensation, 14(b), or uniform minimum wage. The survey makes it particularly clear that younger members and suburban members are a special problem. Wherever and whenever we brought up and discussed a so-called union issue, such as those I've mentioned, the core of the opposition or disinterest was the union member under thirty—and the suburbanite commuter. We've all heard, or even made comments about the lack of understnding of union members...but the fact is...the 60s and 70s are what is right now. And the problems of this and the next

decade seem to bear little, if any relationship to the problems of previous years.[126]

The saga of the Kraft poll marked the end of the 1966 election for the labor movement. The poll indicated that traditional union demands did not inspire or motivate young suburban members. This group was drifting further and further from the central political concerns held by the unions. Attempts to bring these members back into the fold by building suburban COPEs would come to naught.[127]

CONCLUSION

This chapter has reviewed COPE's attempt to aggregate groups into the Democratic party and the problems it encountered in this regard. It demonstrated that organized labor was heavily involved in giving financial, in-kind, and political support to the civil rights movement. This supports the Greenstone-Harrington thesis and contradicts such left-wing critics as Mike Davis and David Milton who dismiss or belittle the AFL-CIO's role in the civil rights movement.[128] But the organizational support COPE gave to civil rights groups had to be done discreetly, through VEP of the Southern Regional Council, Southern state councils, or Phil Weightman's office, because of the opposition such activity stimulated among the local union leadership. COPE could not win them over to its partisan strategy despite its arguments that only employers benefited from the continued division between union members and blacks. COPE lacked the organizational resources to address the race issue directly. It lacked the sanctions (trusteeship) and rewards (a national contract that provided wages above prevailing rates) available to affiliated unions that dared to confront racism among their members. The economistic approach that COPE took to the issue was the only way it could hold the membership together.

But, perhaps, COPE gave up too much by retreating as it did to what it thought would be firmer ground. By failing to contest the race issue directly, it let the opposition define it for the membership. Arguments that civil rights undermined seniority or property values were dismissed, but never answered. Furthermore, the economistic appeals that COPE made in response to the race issue had lost their force among the membership due to demographic changes that had taken place. The Kraft poll indicated that such concerns as those COPE used to divert members from the race issue were, in fact, of little interest to them.

The more issues emerged, like civil rights, outside the economistic framework of COPE's leadership, the more it dug in. Challenged to respond to such issues, COPE clung to economism more tightly. Regardless of the lessons the 1966 campaign had to teach, the following letter from Al Barkan to Barney Weeks indicates the terrain on which COPE would contest future elections:

> It is my feeling that if we can make our [affiliated union] staff people realize that a political defeat in 1968 will be followed by anti-Labor legislation we can get the same involvement in 1968 as we get in right-to-work battles. Our difficulty is in making the staff see the reality and immanence of this danger.
>
> I would appreciate your help in doing everything we can to bring the full impact of the danger we face to the leadership and membership in your state. I am convinced that when they see the reality of this danger we will get activity that we couldn't get otherwise.[129]

NOTES

1. "National Directors Report to the COPE Administrative Commitee" in COPE Research Department Files, Lot 1, Box 3; Folder 31, George Meany Memorial Archives, Silver Springs, Maryland.

2. Lonnie B. Daniel to J. M. Van Houton (March 9, 1961), in Philip Weightman Collection, Robert F. Wagner Labor Archives, New York University, N.Y.

3. Building and Construction Trades Department Convention Proceedings, 1961, 156-60.

4. *Memo From Cope* (August 20, 1961).

5. Dan Powell to Al Barkan (November 23, 1962), in Dan Powell Papers, Folder 197, Southern Historical Collection, Library of the University of North Carolina, Chapel Hill, N.C.

6. Ibid.

7. Ibid.

8. Ibid.

9. Ibid.

10. Ibid.

11. "Field Report," Dan Powell to Jim McDevitt (March 31, 1957), in Dan Powell Papers, Folder 87.

12. "Field Report," Dan Powell to Jim McDevitt (December 18, 1961), in Dan Powell Papers, Folder 196.

13. Ibid.

14. "A Memorandum: The ACWA Affiliation Problem," Claude Ramsay to Dan Powell (August 29, 1962), in Claude Ramsay Papers, Box 13; Folder "ACWA," Southern Labor Archives, Georgia State University, Atlanta, Ga. See also, George H. Kuhndahl, Jr., "Organized Labor in Alabama State Politics," (Ph.D., University of Alabama, 1967), 108 for confirmation of the problem the dues structure called for in Programs of Progress posed for small local unions.

15. George Ellison to Jim McDevitt (March 23, 1962), in Dan Powell Papers, Folder 31.

16. Thomas Knight to Al Barkan (September 9, 1963), in Claude Ramsay Papers, Box 4; Folder "COPE Office Correspondence, 1963-1964."

17. "COPE Program 1966" (n.d.), in Dan Powell Papers, Folder 206.

18. "A Report on the Mississippi AFL-CIO Program of Progress," (December, 1968), in Claude Ramsay Papers, Box 5; Folder, "Affiliated Local Correspondence."

19. "Registration Report for New Jersey," Earl W. Davis to Philip M. Weightman (October, 1961), in possession of Earl Davis, Richmond, Va.

20. "Report of the Central Area Voter Registration Project," Charles Mitchell to Philip M. Weightman (November 15, 1962), in Philip Weightman Collection, Box 6; Folder, "Voter Registration, Ohio."

21. *Washington D.C. Star Press* (September 9, 1962), in COPE Research Department Files, Lot 1, Box 3; Folder 26.

22. "Report on National Democratic Committee and AFL-CIO COPE Conference on Registration" in Philip Weightman Collection, Box 5; Folder, "Cope Conference on Registration."

23. Earl Davis to Jim McDevitt (January 31, 1962), in Philip Weightman Collection.

24. "Report of National Director to COPE Operating Committee" (August 13, 1957), in COPE Research Department files, Lot 1, Box 3;

Folder 31. See also Philip Weightman Collection, Box 1; Folders "Alabama-Local" and "Alabama-State" where arrangements for COPE to assist ASCARV are discussed.

25. Fannie Neal Oral History, Michigan Historical Collections (Bentley Historical Library, University of Michigan), 40-52. See also Philip Weightman Collection, Box 1; Folder, "Alabama-State."

26. Earl Davis to Jim McDevitt, (December 15, 1959), in Dan Powell Papers, Folder 3.

27. Earl Davis to Jim McDevitt, (August 15, 1959), in Dan Powell Papers, Folder 3.

28. Earl Davis to Jim McDevitt, (May 15, 1958), in Dan Powell Papers, Folder 3. See also Philip Weightman Collection, Box 3; Folder "Earl Davis #1."

29. Ray Marshall "Union Racial Problems in the South," *Industrial Relations* 1961. See also material in the Stanton Smith Papers, Box 676, Folder 171, Southern Labor Archives, Georgia State University, Atlanta, Ga. The statement by the Chattanooga local Council retracting their earlier position is reprinted in *Labor World* (September 14, 1955), in the Henry Via Papers, Box 7278; Folder 21, Southern Labor Archives, Georgia State University, Atlanta, Ga.

30. "Field Report," Dan Powell to Jim McDevitt (March 17, 1958), in Dan Powell Papers, Folder 42.

31. "Field Report," Dan Powell to Jim McDevitt (November 30, 1957), in Dan Powell Papers, Folder 42.

32. Ben Williams to Ben Segal (October 11, 1957), Southern Regional Council Collection 75-05/15-04, Atlanta University Center Library, Atlanta, Ga.

33. Kuhndahl, 47.

34. Kuhndahl, p. 47. See also, Marshall *op. cit.*; and Henry L. Trewitt, "Southern Unions and the Integration Issue," *The Reporter* (October 4, 1956): 25-28.

35. *New York Times* (February 26, 1956).

36. Tom Knight to Jim McDevitt (July 5, 1961), in Claude Ramsay Papers, Box 4; Folder "1961—Letters to Affiliated Locals, Executive Board and Building and Trades Council."

37. J. M. Franklin to Claude Ramsay (June 7, 1961), in Claude Ramsay Papers, Box 38; Folder, "Freedom Riders."

38. Claude Ramsay to George Meany (June 9, 1961), in Claude Ramsay Papers, Box 38; Folder "Freedom Riders."

39. *Birmingham Post* (August 25, 1963), in Dan Powell Papers, Folder 206.

40. Marshall *op. cit.*, p. 127-28.

41. These events are described in a "Memo" by Wiley Branton, "Re: New Orleans" (February 20, 1963), in Southern Regional Council Collection, 15-06/04-22, Atlanta University Center Library, Atlanta, Ga.

42. Jim McDevitt to Elliot Gage (July 15, 1963), in Philip Weightman Collection, Box 5; Folder "James L. McDevitt, 1961-1963."

43. Dan Powell to Mr. J. Lebouche, Jr. (January 10, 1958), in Dan Powell Papers, Folder 86.

44. George Ellison to Jim McDevitt, (April 20, 1959), in Dan Powell Papers, Folder 29.

45. Wilbur Hobby to Walter Bartkin, (n.d.), in Dan Powell Papers, Folder 136.

46. George Ellison to Philip Weightman (July 17, 1961), in Philip Weightman Collection, Box 3; Folder "Arkansas State." See also Roy Smithhart to Philip Weightman (September 3, 1959), in Philip Weightman Collection, Box 3; Folder, "Mississippi State."

47. *AFL-CIO News* (September 10, 1966).

48. Donald C. Mosley, "The Labor Movement" in Richard Aubrey McLemore (ed.), *A History of Mississippi* Volume II (Jackson: University and College Press of Mississippi, 1973), 265.

49. Robert S. McElvain, "Claude Ramsay, Organized Labor, and the Civil Rights Movement in Mississippi, 1959-1966," in Merl E. Reed, Leslie S. Hough and Gary M. Fink (eds.) *Southern Workers and Their Unions, 1880-1975* (Westport, Conn.: Greenwood Press, 1981), 110-37.

50. Claude Ramsay Oral History, University of Southern Mississippi, volume 215, 1982, 125.

51. Ibid., 93.

52.   Ibid., 49.

53.   Kuhndahl, 93-98.

54.   Philip Taft, *Organizing Dixie: Alabama Workers in the Industrial Era* (Westport, Conn.: Greenwood Press, 1981), 175. See also *New York Times*, (June 14, 1964) which inaccurately reports that only the Alabama state council experienced significant defections over the race issue.

55.   Barney Weeks to Dan Powell (April 3, 1964), in Dan Powell Papers, Folder 5.

56.   Interview with Barney Weeks, January 7, 1987, Montgomery, Alabama. See also Kuhndahl, 80.

57.   Fannie Neal to Philip Weightman in Philip Weightman Collection.

58.   George Ellison to Dan Powell (October 4, 1961), in Dan Powell Papers, Folder 30.

59.   Dan Powell to Joseph M. Rourke, (May 10, 1965), in Dan Powell Papers, Folder 226.

60.   Mississippi state AFL-CIO Convention Proceedings 1964, 5.

61.   J. B. Williams to Tom Knight (October 3, 1964), in Claude Ramsay Papers, Box 21; Folder "unmarked."

62.   Claude Ramsay to Stanton Smith (July 8, 1964), in Claude Ramsay Papers, Box 10; Folder "AFL-CIO State and Local Central Bodies."

63.   Stanton Smith to International Presidents (June 16, 1965), in Claude Ramsay Papers, Box 10; Folder "AFL-CIO State and Local Central Bodies."

64.   Joseph DePaola to Stanton Smith (June 24, 1965), in Claude Ramsay Papers, Box 10; Folder "AFL-CIO State and Local Central Bodies."

65.   Claude Ramsay to Stanton Smith, (February 11, 1965), in Claude Ramsay Papers, Box 10; Folder "AFL-CIO State and Local Central Bodies."

66. Dan Powell to Joseph M. Rourke (May 10, 1965), in Dan Powell Papers, Folder 30.

67. Claude Ramsay to Al Barkan (November 15, 1965), in Claude Ramsay Papers, Box 13; Folder "Mississippi Voters and Education League."

68. "Minutes of Executive Board Meeting," (March 4, 1966), in Claude Ramsay Papers, Box 36; Folder "1966 Memo File."

69. "VEP Project in Mississippi" in Claude Ramsay Papers, Box 10; Folder "Voter Registration, Organization #2."

70. Aaron Henry to Friends, (April 4, 1966), in Claude Ramsay Papers, Box 4; Folder "1966 Affiliated Local Correspondence."

71. Claude Ramsay to Philip Weightman, (May 13, 1966), in Claude Ramsay Papers, Box 10; Folder "Voter Registration Organization, #1."

72. *Delta Democrat-Times* (May 29, 1966), in Claude Ramsay Papers, Box 33; Folder "1966 Convention Material."

73. Statement from Carpenters local union 2314, IBEW local union 917, Plumbers and Steamfitters local union 123 and Painters local union 433 in Claude Ramsay Papers, Box 10; Folder "Voter Registration Organization, #1."

74. See Letter to the Editor in the *Leader-Call* (May 31, 1966), in Claude Ramsay Papers, Box 10; Folder "Voter Registration, Organization #1."

75. See for example the *Meridean Star* (June 2, 1966), in Claude Ramsay Papers, Box 10; Folder, "Voter Registration, Organization #1."

76. Claude Ramsay to Stanton Smith (June 6, 1966), in Claude Ramsay Papers, Box 10; Folder "AFL-CIO State and Local Central Bodies."

77. "Mississippi AFL-CIO Report" in Claude Ramsay Papers, Box 36; Folder "1966 Memo File."

78. Claude Ramsay to E. S. Jolly in Claude Ramsay Papers, Box 10; Folder "Voter Registration Organization #1."

79. For instance, see the letter from Claude Ramsay to Amizie Moore (October 20, 1967), in Claude Ramsay Papers, Box 10; Folder "Voter Registration Organization #1."

80. Aaron Henry to Claude Ramsay (November 26, 1966), in Claude Ramsay Papers, Box 10; Folder "Voter Registration Organization #1."

81. For example see the letters from Darsey Lewis to Claude Ramsay (July 18, 1966), or John Buffington to Claude Ramsay (September 20, 1966), in Claude Ramsay Papers, Box 10; Folder "Voter Registration Organization #1."

82. Victor Bussie to Emory Via (April 20, 1966), in Southern Regional Council Collection, Box 1, Folder 21, Atlanta University, Atlanta, Ga.

83. George Ellison to Al Barkan (January 22, 1964), in Dan Powell Papers, Folder 32.

84. "Matching Grants Report," Dan Powell to Joseph P. Rourke (May 10, 1965), in Dan Powell Papers, Folder 204.

85. Dr. R. A. Hawkins to Daniel Powell (May 4, 1964), in Dan Powell Papers Collection, Folder 135.

86. Interview with Claude Ramsay, December 27, 1985, "Inquiry," WLBT, T.V. 3, Jackson, Ms. See also Claude Ramsay's Oral History, *op. cit.*, 49.

87. Fannie Neal Oral History, *op. cit.*, 85. See also Fannie Neal to Alexander Barkan (n.d.) and Earl Davis to Al Barkan (April 3, 1964), in Philip Weightman Collection, Box 7; Folder "Voter Registration-Oklahoma."

88. *Tulsa Tribune* (May 6, 1964), in Claude Ramsay Papers, Box 10; Folder "COPE Office Correspondence."

89. "AFL-CIO COPE Schedule: Contributions, Jan. 1, 1964 to December 31, 1964," in possession of the author.

90. Herbert Harris, "The Riddle of the Labor Vote," *Harper's Magazine* (October 1964): 43-44.

91. "What the Unions Did to Help Elect the Democrats," *U.S. News and World Report* (November 9, 1964): 102-5.

92. *AFL-CIO News* (December 1, 1964).

93. "Special Allocations, 1960-1962-1964," in possession of author.

94. Kentucky state Convention Proceedings, 1964, 37.

95. "Liberals Gain among Candidates Backed by COPE," *Congressional Quarterly Weekly Report* (November 13, 1964): 2681.

96. *Memo From COPE* (November 1, 1965).

97. AFL-CIO Convention Proceedings, Vol. II, 1965, 1-6.

98. Willard Shelton, "New Factors in the 1966 Election," *American Federationist* (February, 1966): 4.

99. *AFL-CIO News* (May 28, 1966).

100. *Memo From COPE* (April 4, 1966).

101. *Washington Daily News* (June 7, 1966).

102. Helmuth Kern to Sir and Brother (April 13, 1967), in Dan Powell Papers, Folder 205.

103. "What the Unions Are Doing to Elect Their Friends," *U.S. News and World Report* (October 24, 1966): 112.

104. Papermakers and Paperworkers Convention Proceedings, 1966, 166-67.

105. International Chemical Workers Union Convention Proceedings, 1966, 363.

106. California Labor COPE Pre-Primary Convention Proceedings, 1966, 5-15.

107. Alabama State Council Convention Proceedings, 1966, 81.

108. Abel's letter is reprinted in *Herling's Labor Letter* (October 29, 1966).

109. *Memo From COPE* (October 17, 1966).

110. "Field Activities Report," Daniel Powell to Joseph P. Rourke (December 3, 1966), in Dan Powell Papers, Folder 206.

111. "COPE Program, 1966," in Dan Powell Papers, Folder 206.

112. "Politics: The White Backlash," *U.S. News and World Report* (October 10, 1966): 27-28.

113. *New York Times* (October 22, 1966).

114. *Labor News* (November 4, 1966).

115. *New York Times* (November 9, 1966).

116. Helmuth Kern to Sir and Brother (April 13, 1967), *op. cit.*

117. "1966 Elections," *COPE Research Department*, in possession of author.

118. Ibid.

119. Al Barkan to Roy Wilkins (December 2, 1966), in Philip Weightman Collection, Box 5; Folder "Al Barkan."

120. These reports and Kern's summary appear in Kern's letter, *op. cit.*

121. Report of the International Labor Press Association to the COPE Operating Committee (January 24, 1967), in possession of the author.

122. John Kraft to Al Barkan (April 24, 1967), in possession of author.

123. *Wall Street Journal* (July 6, 1967).

124. Al Barkan, "The Union Member: Profile an Attitudes," *American Federationist* (August 1967): 1.

125. See the article by Edward J. Carlough, in the *Sheet Metal Workers Journal* in COPE Research Department files, Lot 1, Box 2; Folder 22.

126. John Kraft to Al Barkan (April 24, 1967), in possession of the author.

127. Dan Powell to Al Barkan (August 10, 1967), in Dan Powell Papers, Folder 42 describes the problems COPE encountered in trying to build suburban COPEs to appeal to young, home owning union members.

128.   Mike Davis, "The Barren Marriage of American Labor and the Democratic Party," *New Left Review* (November 1980): 84; David Milton, *The Politics of U.S. Labor: From the Great Depression to the New Deal* (N.Y.: Monthly Review Press, 1982), 165.

129.   Al Barkan to Barney Weeks (August 24, 1967), in Dan Powell Papers.

Conclusion

The AFL-CIO engaged in social democratic activity, organizing groups beyond the union membership into the Democratic party, in pursuit of thoroughly pluralistic goals: to ensure a favorable environment in which to conduct collective bargaining. Such partisan activity was necessary once the conditions surrounding collective bargaining had been politicized. Politicization of collective bargaining took two forms. First, it took the form of political regulation of labor-management relations. This occurred through such legislation as the National Labor Relations Act, Taft-Hartley amendments stiffening this legislation, and then in 1959 the Landrum-Griffin Act. Such legislation meant that the relative political capacities of labor and capital would determine the economic resources each group could utilize in collective bargaining. In an essay entitled "Why Labor is in Politics" McDevitt wrote:

> No matter how you look at it...the American Labor movement just did not have any choice; whether they [sic] like it or not they are compelled to get into this thing [electoral politics], to give it everything they have to protect our interests in the economic field.[1]

Under such circumstances, the unions increasingly identified defense of their economic resources with the Democratic party and mobilized groups outside the union membership into it in order to ensure the Party's success.

A second factor that contributed to the politicization of collective bargaining was increasing state regulation of the economy. Political regulation of the economy determined the economic as opposed to legal environment in which collective bargaining would take place. Roy

Reuther told the delegates to the 1964 Colorado state council convention:

> You don't negotiate a contract, brothers and sisters, in a vacuum. When there are hard times...it is pretty tough to negotiate a decent contract....I have negotiated at the bargaining table and I can tell you the best kind of condition to negotiate a contract is when there is full employment, when things are booming, when there's big purchasing power.[2]

Thus, political influences increasingly intruded on the market strategies of the affiliated unions. Such influences conditioned the economic environment in which collective bargaining would take place, structured the conduct of the parties in collective bargaining, and determined the resources each side could mobilize legally in defense of their market objectives. Pomper writes, "In contrast to previous years, labor organizations today are continually concerned with their influence upon government and its effect upon them. This concern derives not from a political orientation inherent in unionism, but from the need for unions to extend their efforts if they are to protect the central core of their interests, the job."[3]

It was this issue, the politicization of collective bargaining and not social welfare demands as Greenstone suggests, that led COPE to aggregate groups outside the membership into the Democratic party. But COPE's partisan strategy was greeted with indifference and even hostility by the very people charged to implement it, the local union leadership. One union report on race relations stated, "The official policy of the labor movement has, for the most part, been clear and unequivocal: the implementation of that policy, however, has often been frustrated by the prevailing attitudes and inaction at the lower levels of the union structure."[4] In lieu of direct threats to their market interests, local union leaders had little interest in bringing blacks into the Party. In addition, racism within the rank and file undermined the alliance with blacks within the Democratic party that COPE hoped to create. If COPE was to implement its strategy it would have to do so without the cooperation of the local union leadership. This COPE proceeded to do. It channeled money covertly through the Southern Regional Council, through Southern state councils, and through Phil Weightman's office to black voter registration groups. In this way COPE hoped to defeat the conservative coalition in Congress that was responsible for thwarting labor's market objectives.

Throughout the text we have given considerable emphasis to the organizational constraints under which COPE had to act. The decentralization of authority and resources within the AFL-CIO prevented COPE from diverging greatly from the market interests of the affiliated unions. COPE received cooperation from the affiliated unions only when their institutional interests were threatened. Otherwise, COPE found it difficult to inspire and organize broad support among the affiliated unions and their locals.

Organizational structures do not simply emerge but reflect strategic choices. Leaders create organizational forms which they believe will permit them to achieve their goals. The organizational structure of the AFL-CIO, its decentralization of authority and resources, followed from the market strategy the American labor movement adopted. It is, ultimately, this market strategy that best explains the partial equivalence that Greenstone found between union-party relations in the United States and those found among social democratic labor movements in Western Europe.[5] The market strategy frustrated the social democratic objectives and activities that the AFL-CIO wished to pursue in two ways.

First, pursuit of a market strategy undermined the programmatic basis upon which a black-labor coalition could be forged. Going through collective bargaining to achieve such typical welfare state benefits as health or old age insurance created consumption cleavages between union members and the very groups COPE was trying to aggregate into the Party. The private welfare state that developed under collective bargaining prevented a classwide outlook—based upon government programs the working class as a whole had an interest in defending—from developing among union members, and between them and blacks.[6]

Secondly, labor movements that pursue a market strategy tend to have decentralized control structures. This decentralization of authority and resources forces the trade union federation to appeal to the mutual self-interest of the affiliated unions in narrow organizational objectives if the federation is to gain their cooperation and support. This is true not only of the AFL-CIO as we have shown, but of other decentralized trade union movements as well. Heidenheimer has noted that in Britain, "The undernourishment of the T.U.C. and related central structures has resulted in limiting the consensus overlap among the demands of the various unions to maintenance of traditional demands that have been hallowed for several generations."[7] The traditional demands to which Heidenheimer refers are organizational demands. Dahl has also noted that decentralized control structures inhibit the pursuit of broad, class demands and that they further narrow interests. He writes, "decentralized bargaining structures strengthen incentives to advance particular interests and weakens incentives to advance more general interests."[8] Decentralization, thus, inhibited COPE from appealing to the membership on the basis of demands that could forge a sense of shared purposes with groups beyond the union membership.

For these reasons, the market strategy, which now required broad electoral support to defend its premises, undermined the very conditions that could create such support. It created consumption cleavages that divided union members from other members of the social democratic constituency and it required a decentralized control structure that engendered narrow interest group appeals.

If COPE is to provide the financial, organizational, and ideological support required to build a social democratic coalition within the Democratic party, the AFL-CIO will first have to alter its conflict strategy. It will have to rely more on legislation than collective bargaining as its preferred means of redistributing the national income. This would require the AFL-CIO to concentrate resources and authority in the central federation and free COPE from its dependence on the affiliated unions. The AFL-CIO will have to adopt an organizational form that is congruent with its new goal.[9]

Whether the AFL-CIO will reshuffle its present mix of conflict strategies, now so weighted toward the market arena, remains to be seen. Conditions exist presently that could provoke such a reassessment. Previously, regular wage and fringe benefit increases could be funded from expanding corporate profits. American businesses could satisfy wage and benefit requests in collective bargaining without endangering their competitive position. Today, this is no longer true. Japan and Western Europe have closed the "technology gap" that formerly provided American business with its competitive advantage.[10] The well of corporate profits that used to fund regular wage and benefit increases has dried up. The economic support of a market strategy—the market power of American business—has collapsed.

Even the most cynical view of union leaders, that union leaders are interested only in their jobs and their members' dues, would seem to favor a reassessment of conflict strategies. Real wages in 1985 were ten percent lower than they were in 1978. Union density has declined. In 1977, for the first time since the New Deal, union membership actually decreased in absolute numbers. And the prospect of enrolling new members does not look encouraging. Fewer representation elections are being held and the unions now lose more of such elections than they win. Even on its own terms the market strategy has not delivered. If recent trends are any indication of the future, continued adherence to a market strategy jeopardizes the very jobs and union treasuries union leaders are so anxious to protect.

But the ability of organizations to resist change is extraordinary even in the face of evidence that current strategies do not work. One need only recall that despite three years of mass unemployment and a sizable loss of members during the Depression, the AFL still opposed unemployment insurance, condemned social security, and only tepidly supported the Wagner Act.[11] There are three reasons why the AFL-CIO might choose the path of least resistance and continue to adhere to a market strategy even though the circumstances that favor such a strategy are eroding.

First, the leadership may be too insecure to shift to a political strategy in which their particular talents are not as highly valued and their personal background acquits them with little experience.[12]

Secondly, a political strategy threatens the authority the affiliated unions now enjoy within the AFL-CIO. The concentration of authority and resources in the central federation that a political strategy requires would come at the expense of the affiliated unions.

Lastly, a market strategy has its own momentum that may prevent it from being cast aside. Members have built up a pattern of interests under the present strategy that they may not be willing to jeopardize.

The future of COPE hangs in the balance of the choice that organized labor now confronts: whether to adhere to a market strategy or pursue a more political, state-oriented approach. This choice will determine whether COPE will continue to respond to the blows the labor movement receives instead of the dreams that it has.[13]

NOTES

1. James McDevitt, "Why Labor Is in Politics," *Speaker's Handbook, 1960* (Washington, D.C.: AFL-CIO, 1960), 53-54.

2. Colorado state AFL-CIO Convention Proceedings, 1964, 175.

3. Gerald Pomper, "Organized Labor in Politics: The Campaign to Revise the Taft-Hartley Act," (Ph.d., Princeton University, 1959), 40.

4. Ronald Donovan, "The Southern Union Staff Training Institute: A Report and Evaluation Prepared for the National Institute of Labor Education," in Henry Via Papers, Box 1278; Folder 19, Southern Labor Archives, Georgia State University, Atlanta, Georgia.

5. J. David Greenstone. *Labor in American Politics* 2nd Ed., (Chicago: University of Chicago Press, 1977), 365.

6. For a discussion of consumption cleavages see Patrick Dunleavy, "The Urban Basis of Political Alignment: Social Class, Domestic Property and Stage Intervention in Consumption Processes," *British Journal of Political Science* (October 1979): 409-45. See also the discussion of such cleavages in Gosta Esping-Anderson, *Politics Against Markets* (Princeton: Princeton University Press), 1985.

7. Arnold Heidenheimer, "Trade Unions, Benefit Systems and Party Mobilization Styles: "Horizontal" Influences on the British Labour and German Social Democratic Parties," *Comparative Politics* (April 1969): 341.

8. Robert Dahl, *Dilemmas of Pluralist Democracy: Autonomy vs Control* (New Haven: Yale University Press, 1982), 73.

9.   David Brody makes a similar point with regard to the old AFL not being structured in such a manner as to engage in politics effectively.   The AFL attempted to intervene in the 1906 congressional elections says Brody but, "No internal reform was undertaken that would have given labor's political arms—the city centrals, the state federations, the AFL itself—the means to do effective political work."   Brody then goes on to explain, "The labor movement had not, of course, intended to make its way by political means.   The focus was unremittingly econoimc, and this orientation determined its structure and strategy."   David Brody, *Workers in Industrial America* (New York: Oxford University Press, 1980), 28.

10.   Ernest Mandel, *Europe vs America: Contraditions in Imperialism* (New York: Monthly Review Press, 1970).

11.   Ruth Horowitz, *The Political Ideologies of Organized Labor: The New Deal Era* (New Brunswick, N.J.:   Transaction Books, 1978), 121-47.

12.   David Brody, "The Expansion of the Labor Movement: Institutional Sources of Stimulus and Constrant" in David Brody (ed.), *The American Labor Movement* (New York: Harper & Row, 1971), 119-35.

13.   This is a paraphrase of a pithy expression in Marc Karson, *American Labor Unions and Politics, 1900-1918* (Carbondale, Ill.: University of Southern Illinois Press, 1958), 40.

Bibliography

Archival Collections

COPE Research Department files.   George Meany Memorial Archives, Silver Springs, Md.

Kroll, Jack. Papers.   Library of Congress, Manuscripts Division, Washington, D.C.

Powell, Dan. Papers.   Southern Historical Collection, Library of the University of North Carolina, Chapel Hill, N.C.

Ramsay, Claude. Papers.   Southern Labor Archives, Georgia State University, Atlanta, Ga.

Southern Regional Council Collection.   Atlanta University Library Center, Atlanta, Ga.

Smith, Stanton. Papers.   Southern Labor Archives, Georgia State University, Atlanta, Ga.

Via, Henry. Papers.   Southern Labor Archives, Georgia State University, Atlanta, Ga.

Weightman, Philip M. Papers.   Robert F. Wagner Labor Archives, New York University, N.Y.

Articles

Allen, V. L. "The Centennial of the British T.U.C.: 1868-1968." in John Saville and Ralph Miliband, eds. *Socialist Register, 1968.* New York: Monthly Review Press, 1968.

Anderson, Totten J. "The 1958 Election in California." *Western Political Quarterly* (March 1959).

Barkan, Al. "The Union Member: Profile and Attitudes." *American Federationist* (August 1967).

Blume, Norman. "The Impact of a Local Union on its Membership in a Local Election." *Western Political Quarterly* (1970), 22 (1).

Brody, David. "Career Requirements and American Trade Unionism." in Leo Jaher, ed. *Age of Industrialism in America.* New York: Free Press, 1969.

-----. "The Expansion of the Labor Movement: Institutional Sources of Stimulus and Constraint." in David Brody, ed., *The American Labor Movement.* New York: Harper & Row, 1971.

Bruner, Dick. "Labor Should Get Out of Politics." *Harper's Magazine* 217 (April 1958).

The Building and Construction Trades Bulletin. "The Need for Union Members to Register and Vote." (August 16, 1960).

Business Week. "Labor's Problems: Laws and Leaders." (November 15, 1952).

-----. "Industry Speaks Up." (April 18, 1953).

-----. "Labor is Seeing Democratic." (October 2, 1954).

-----. "Labor Goes on the Political Defensive." (October 18, 1958).

-----. "Unions Enter Political Arena With Drive to Get Out the Vote." (August 27, 1960).

Congressional Quarterly Weekly Report. "Liberals Gain among Candidates Backed by COPE." (November 13, 1964).

Davis, Mike. "The Barren Marriage of American Labor and the Democratic Party." *New Left Review* (November 1980).

Dawson, Andrew. "The Paradox of Dynamic Technological Change and the Labour Aristocracy in the United States." *Labor History* 20 (Summer 1979).

Dunleavy, Patrick. "The Urban Basis of Political Alignment: Social Class, Domestic Property and State Intervention in Consumption Process." *British Journal of Political Science* (October 1979).

Fink, Gary M. "The Rejection of Voluntarism." *Industrial and Labor Relations Review* 26 (January 1973).

Foner, Eric. "Why is There No Socialism in the United States?" *History Workshop Journal* #17.

Fortune. "Labor." (November 1956).

Fuchs, Ralph. "The Hearing Examiner Fiasco Under the Administrative Procedures Act." *Harvard Law Review* 63 (March 1950).

Harris, Herbert. "The Riddle of the Labor Vote." *Harper's Magazine* (October 1964).

Heidenheimer, Arnold. "Trade Unions, Benefit Systems and Party Mobilization Styles: "Horizontal" Influences on the British Labor and German Social Democratic Parties." *Comparative Politics* (April 1969).

Hester, Frank. "Ohio Labor and Political Action." *Political Affairs* 41 (November 1962).

Holloway, Harry. "Interest Groups in the Post-Partisan Era: The Political Machine of the AFL-CIO." *Political Science Quarterly.* Vol. 94 (Spring 1979).

Hutchinson, John. "The Constitution and Government of the AFL-CIO." *California Law Review.* Vol. 46 (1958).

Katznelson, Ira. "Considerations on Social Democracy in the United States." *Comparative Politics.* Vol. 11 (October 1978).

Klare, Karl E. "Judicial Deradicalization of the Wagner Act and the Origins of Modern Legal Consciousness, 1937-1941." *Minnesota Law Review* 62 (March 1978).

Lipset, Seymour Martin. "Why No Socialism in the U.S.?" in S. Bailer and S. Sluzar, eds. *Sources of Contemporary Radicalism.* Boulder: Westview Press, 1977.

Marshall, F. Ray. "Union Racial Problems in the South." *Industrial Relations* (1961).

McDevitt, James L. "The People Are Deeply Concerned." *American Federationist* (August 1958).

-----. "The People Do Alright." *American Federationist* (December 1958).

-----. "Why Labor Is In Politics." *Speaker's Handbook, 1960.* Washington, D.C.: AFL-CIO, 1960.

McDevitt, James L. and Jack Kroll. "Give COPE Your Support." *American Federationist* (May 1956).

McElvain, Robert S. "Claude Ramsay, Organized Labor, and the Civil Rights Movement in Mississippi, 1959-1966." in Merl E. Reed, Leslie S. Hough and Gary M. Fink, eds. *Southern Workers and Their Unions, 1880-1975.* Westport, Conn.: Greenwood Press, 1981.

Meany, George. "Don't Force American Labor to Start a Political Party." *Commercial and Financial Chronicle* (January 15, 1959).

Miller, Glenn W. and Stephen B. Ware. "Organized Labor in the Political Process: A Case Study of the Right-to-work Campaign in Ohio." *Labor History* (Winter 1963).

Mosley, Donald C. "The Labor Movement." In Richard McLemore, ed. *A History of Mississippi,* Vol. 2. Jackson: University and College Press of Mississippi, 1973.

The Nation. "The Merger: Credits and Debits." (December 10, 1955).

Perlman, Selig. "Labor and the New Deal in Historical Perspective." in Milton Derber and Edwin Young, eds. *Labor and the New Deal.* Madison: University of Wisconsin Press, 1957.

Perlman, Selig and William H. Knowles. "American Unionism in the Postwar World." in T.C.T. McCormick, ed. *Problems of the Postwar World.* New York: McGraw-Hill, 1945.

Pomper, Gerald. "Labor Legislation: The Revision of Taft-Hartley in 1953-1954," *Labor History* 6 (Spring 1965).

Rehmus, Charles M. "Labor in American Politics." in William Haber, ed. *Labor in a Changing America.* New York: Basic Books, 1966.

Rogin, Michael Paul. "Voluntarism: The Political Functions of an Antipolitical Doctrine." *Industrial and Labor Relations Review* 15 (July 1962).

Scher, Seymour. "Regulatory Agency Control Trhough Appointment: The Case of the Eisenhower Administration." *The Journal of Politics* 23 (November 1961).

Scoble, Harry M. "Organized Labor in Electoral Politics: The State of the Discipline." *Western Political Quarterly* Vol. 14 (September 1963).

Seidman, Joel. "Efforts Toward Merger, 1935-1955." *Industrial and Labor Relations Review* (April 1956).

Shelton, Willard. "New Factors in the 1966 Election." *The American Federationist* (February 1966).

Stephens, John D. "Class Formation and Class Consciousness: A Statistical and Empirical Analysis With Reference to Britain and Sweden." *British Journal of Sociology* Vol. 30 (December 1979).

Svirdorf, Mitchell. "The Responsibility of Union Officers in Politics." in *Workers as Union Members, Consumers and as Citizens*, Bulletin No. 31. Minneapolis: Minnesota School of Industrial Relations, 1961.

Trewitt, Henry L. "Southern Unions and the Integration Issue." *The Reporter* (October 4, 1956).

U.S. News and World Report. "Union Warfare on the Horizon." (April 10, 1952).

-----. "How Unions Came Out in the Election." (November 16, 1956).

-----. "What Happened in the Election?" (November 14, 1958).

-----. "'Why I Won'-'Why I Lost.'" (November 14, 1958).

-----. "Inside Story: Why It Wasn't Nixon." (January 30, 1961).

-----. "What the Unions Did to Help Elect the Democrats." (November 9, 1964).

-----. "Politics: The White Blacklash." (October 10, 1966).

-----. "What the Unions Are Doing to Elect Their Friends." (October 24, 1966).

Wilentz, Sean. "Against Exceptionalism: Class Consciousness and the American Labor Movement, 1790-1920." *International Labor and Working Class History* No. 26 (Fall 1984).

Wirtz, W. Willard. "The New N.L.R.B.: Herein of Employer Persuasion," *Northwestern Law Review* 49 (1955).

Books

Aronowitz, Stanley. *False Promises: The Shaping of American Working Class Consciousness*. New York: McGraw-Hill, 1973.

Bernstein, Irving. *The Lean Years*. Boston: Houghton, Mifflin, 1960.

Bullard, Todd. *Labor and the Legislature*. Morgantown, W.V.: Bureau for Government Research, 1965.

Clegg, Hugh. *Trade Unionism Under Collective Bargaining: A Theory Based on a Comparison of Six Countries*. Oxford: B. Blackwell, 1976.

Cook, Stephen L. *What is the Impact of State and Local Central Body Endorsement on the Rank and File*. Morgantown, W.V.: Institute for Labour Studies, 1975.

Dahl, Robert. *Dilemmas of Pluralist Democracy: Autonomy vs Control*. New Haven: Yale University Press, 1982.

Dubofsky, Melvin and Warren Van Tine. *John L. Lewis*. New York: Quadrangle Books, 1977.

Esping-Anderson, Gosta. *Politics Against Markets*. Princeton: Princeton University Press, 1985.

Fenno, Richard. *Congressmen in Committees*. Boston: Little, Brown & Co., 1973.

Fink, Gary (ed.) *AFL-CIO Executive Council Statements and Reports, 1965-1975*, Vol. 1. Westport, Conn.: Greenwood Press, 1977.

Form, William. *Divided We Stand: Working Class Stratification in America*. Urbana: University of Illinois Press, 1985.

Foster, James C. *The Union Politic: The C.I.O. Political Action Committee*. Columbia: University of Missouri Press, 1975.

Godson, Roy. *American Labor and European Politics: The A.F.L. as a Transnational Force*. New York: Crane-Russak, 1976.

Goldberg, Arthur. *Labor United*. N.Y.: McGraw-Hill, 1956.

Goulden, Joseph. *Meany*. N.Y.: Atheneum, 1972.

Greenstone, J. David. *Labor in American Politics*, 2nd ed. Chicago: University of Chicago Press, 1977.

Harrington, Michael. *Socialism.* New York: Saturday Review Press, 1973.

Hartz, Louis. *The Liberal Tradition in America.* New York: Harcourt, Brace & World, 1955.

Higgins, George. *Voluntarism in Organized Labor in the United States, 1930-1940.* New York: Arno Press, 1969.

Hirsh, Susan. *Roots of the American Working Class: The Industrialization of Crafts in Newark, 1800-1860.* Philadelphia: University of Pennsylvania Press, 1978.

Horowitz, Ruth. *Political Ideologies of Organized Labor: The New Deal Era.* New Brunswick, N.J.: Transcation Books, 1978.

Kahn, Melvin. *The Politics of American Labor: The Indiana Microcosm.* Carbondale: Southern Illinois University Labor Institute, 1970.

Karson, Marc. *American Labor and Politics, 1900-1918.* Carbondale: Southern Illinois University Press, 1958.

Lenin, Vladimir. *What Is To Be Done?* New York: International Publishers, 1973.

MacAdams, Carl. *Power and Politics in Labor Legislation.* New York: Columbia University Press, 1974.

Mandel, Ernest. *Europe vs America: Contradiction in Imperialism.* New York: Monthly Review Press, 1970.

McConnell, Grant. *Private Power and American Democracy.* New York: Knopf, 1966.

Milton, David. *The Politics of U.S. Labor: From the Great Depression to the New Deal.* New York: Monthly Review Press, 1982.

Mink, Gwendolyn. *Old Labor and New Immigrants in American Political Development.* Ithaca: Cornell University, 1986.

Oshinsky, David. *Senator Joseph McCarthy and the American Labor Movement.* Columbia: University of Missouri Press, 1976.

Palmer, Kenneth. *State Politics in the United States.* New York: St. Martin's Press, 1970.

Pelling, Henry. *American Labor.* Chicago: University of Chicago Press, 1960.

-----. *The Origins of the Labour Party.* Oxford: Clarendon Press, 1965.

Perlman, Selig. *A Theory of the Labor Movement.* New York: MacMillan, 1928.

Reed, Louis. *The Labor Philosophy of Samuel Gompers.* New York: Columbia University Press, 1930.

Reichard, Gary. *The Reaffirmation of Republicanism* Knoxville: University of Tennessee Press, 1975.

Selznick, Philip. *T.V.A. and the Grass Roots.* Berkeley: University of California Press, 1949.

Sombart, Werner. *Why is There No Socialism in the United States?* White Plains, N.Y.: Sharp Publishers, 1976.

Taft, Philip. *The A.F. of L. in the Time of Gompers.* New York: Harper & Row, 1957.

-----. *The A.F. of L. From the Death of Gompers to the Merger.* New York: Harper & Row, 1959.

-----. *Labor Politics American Style: The California State Federation of Labor.* Cambridge: Harvard University Press, 1968.

-----. *Organizing Dixie: Alabama Workers in the Industrial Era.* Westport, Conn.: Greenwood Press, 1981.

Velie, Lester. *Labor, U.S.A.* New York: Harper and Row, 1959.

Ware, Norman. *The Labor Movement in the United States, 1865-1890.* Gloucester, Mass.: P. Smith, 1959.

Webb, Beatrice and Sidney Webb. *Industrial Democracy.* London: Longman's, Green & Co., 1926.

Wilson, James Q. *Political Organizations.* New York: Basic Books, 1974).

Government Documents

Federal Trade Commission, *Quarterly Financial Reports*, 1947-1969, Washington, D.C.: U.S. Government Printing Office.

U.S. Bureau of Labor Statistics. "Measures of Compensation, 1972." Washington, D.C.: Department of Labor, 1972.

U.S. Department of Labor, Annual Report of the NLRB, Washington, D.C.: Dept. of Labor, 1952-56.

U.S. Department of Labor, *Labor Organizations Annual Report*, Contributions, Gifts, and Grants, Form L-M II, Schedule 12, 1980.

U.S. Senate Committee on Labor and Public Welfare. *Hearings on Taft-Hartley Revisions*, 83rd Cong., 1st Sess.

Interviews and Oral Histories

Barkan, Al. November 22, 1979: Washington, D.C.

Murray, Henry. April 22, 1979: New Haven, Ct.

Neal, Fannie. Oral History. Michigan Historical Collections, Bentley Historical Library, University of Michigan, Ann Arbor, Mi.

Powell, Dan. January 23, 1981: Memphis, Tenn.

Ramsay, Claude. December 27, 1985: "Inquiry," WLBT T.V. 3, Jackson, Miss.

-----. Oral History. University of Southern Mississippi, Vol. 215, 1982.

Weeks, Barney. January 7, 1987: Montgomery, Ala.

Labor Publications and Convention Proceedings

AFL Convention Proceedings, 1952-55.

AFL-CIO Convention Proceedings, 1957-65.

Alabama Labor Council Special Convention Proceedings, 1958.

Alabama State Council Convention Proceedings, 1966.

Building and Construction Trades Convention Proceedings, 1959-61.

California Labor COPE Pre-Primary Convention Proceedings, 1962-69.

"Can You Talk About Race Without Losing Your Temper." Washington, D.C.: COPE, 1966.

CIO Convention Proceedings, 1954.

Colorado State AFL-CIO Convention Proceedings, 1964.

"How to Win." (Washington, D.C.: AFL-CIO, 1964).

Idaho State AFL-CIO Convention Proceedings, 1974.

Industrial Unions Department Convention Proceedings, 1957.

International Chemical Workers Convention Proceedings, 1966.

Kansas Federation of Labor Convention Proceedings, 1960.

Kentucky State AFL-CIO Convention Proceedings, 1964-70.

Maryland State and D.C. AFL-CIO Convention Proceedings, 1965-69.

Mississippi State AFL-CIO Convention Proceedings, 1964.

Papermakers and Paperworkers Convention Proceedings, 1966.

Pulp, Paper and Sulphite Workers Convention Proceedings, 1956.

"The Vital Links." AFL-CIO, n.d.

United Automobile, Aerospace and Agricultural Implements Workers of America Convention Proceedings, 1953.

Newspapers

AFL-CIO News.

Herling's Labor Letter.

Labor News.

Memo From COPE.

New York Times.

Wall Street Journal.

Washington Daily News.

Unpublished Masters Thesis and Dissertations

Gall, Gilbert. "Sterile Combat: Labor Politics and Right-to-Work." Unpublished Dissertation, Wayne State University, 1984.

Kuhndahl Jr., George H. "Organized Labor in Alabama State Politics." Unpublished Dissertation, University of Alabama, 1967.

Pomper, Gerald. "Organized Labor in Politics: The Campaign to Revise the Taft-Hartley Act." Unpublished Dissertation, Princeton University, 1959.

Scott, Ebbin Pina. "The AFL-CIO Merger: Unity and Accomplishments." Unpublished Masters thesis, University of Maryland, 1961.

Wolpin, Miles. "Factors Influencing Labor's Internal Political Cohesion." Unpublished Masters thesis, Columbia University, 1964.

Index

Abel, I.W., 122 affiliates: and class issues, 4, 45; and collective bargaining, 20, 62-63, 94; conventions of, 37; COPE relations with, 3-8, 44, 54, 66, 75, 77, 94, 100-101, 140-41, 142; and the elections of the 1950s, 66, 67; and the elections of the 1960s, 79, 117, 118, 120; endorsements by, 4; and financial contributions, 66, 74, 75, 79, 86, 91, 93, 121; and the Landrum-Griffin Act, 8, 75; and local organizations, 67, 75; and market strategy, 55, 140, 143; political activity of, 3-4, 32, 100; and political education, 60, 74, 77; and racism, 128; self interest of, 5; and social democracy, 56; and social issues, 14, 56; and union security, 60, 73; and voluntarism, 14

AFL [American Federation of Labor]: "Bill of Grievances" of the, 15-16; conventions, 32, 36, 37-38; decentralized structure of the, 55; endorsements by the, 17; financial contributions of the 62, 66, 85, 93; as national spokesman for labor, 30; political activity of the, 12-21; and the politicizing of labor policy, 27; and social issues, 15; and the Taft-Hartley Act [1947], 27, 30-32; and the Wagner Act, 27. See also AFL-CIO; voluntarism

AFL-CIO: conventions, 46, 47-48, 73-74, 75, 77, 119-20; goals of, 139; merger, 7, 29-30, 33-39, 46-47, 55, 61, 62, 64-67, 73. See also name of specific state, topic or individual

Agnew, Spiro, 121

Alabama, 36, 101, 103, 105, 106, 107-8, 111, 112, 115, 117, 122

Alexandria, Louisiana, 108

Amalgamated Clothing Workers Union, 47, 52, 104

Amalgamated Meatcutters, 49, 51, 124-25

American exceptionalism, 2

American Federation of Labor. See AFL; AFL-CIO

anti-labor legislation: and collective bargaining, 6, 17-19, 26; and cooperation with COPE, 101; and elections in the 1960s, 122, 129; and Programs of Progress, 104; and state legislatures, 29, 36-37, 38, 67-68, 139-40; and voluntarism, 6, 12-15. See also name of specific piece of legislation or individual

Arkansas, 101, 103-4, 107, 110, 111, 112-13, 115, 123

Asbestos Workers union, 80-81

Austin, Richard B., 65

Auto Workers, 29, 52, 55, 80, 91, 106, 108, 120

Ayers, William, 78

backlash, white, 123-24

Baltimore, Maryland, 80, 92, 93, 121

Barkan, Al, 61, 66, 101, 108-9, 118, 121-22, 123, 124, 126, 127, 128-29

Bass, Ross, 121

Beck, Dave, 63, 64

Beeson, Albert C., 34

Bennett, Wallace, 63

Bernstein, Irving, 19

"Bill of Grievances" [AFL], 15-16

About the Author

ALAN DRAPER is Associate Professor of Government and Coordinator of the Work and Society Program at St. Lawrence University. He grew up in New York City, attended the University of Wisconsin as an undergraduate, and received his Ph.D. from Columbia University in 1982. His reviews and articles have appeared in the *American Political Science Review*, *Economic and Industrial Democracy*, and *Labor History*. His current research is on the role organized labor played in the civil rights movement.